FIRST LADY

MICHAEL ASHCROFT

FIRST LADY

INTRIGUE AT THE COURT OF
CARRIE AND BORIS JOHNSON

Biteback Publishing

First published in Great Britain in 2022 by
Biteback Publishing Ltd, London
Copyright © Michael Ashcroft 2022

ISBN 978-1-78590-750-0

10 9 8 7 6 5 4 3 2 1

A CIP catalogue record for this book is available from the British Library.

Set in Minion and Avenir

Printed and bound in Great Britain by
CPI Group (UK) Ltd, Croydon CR0 4YY

CONTENTS

AUTHOR'S ROYALTIES

Lord Ashcroft is donating all author's royalties from *First Lady* to charities supporting the NHS.

ACKNOWLEDGEMENTS

Among the scores of people who kindly agreed to be interviewed for this book, many asked not to be named publicly. For this reason, it is not possible to identify here everybody who deserves thanks; suffice it to say that without their input this project would not have been possible. For ease of reference, it should be assumed that unless otherwise attributed all quotes are taken from interviews conducted for this book between July 2021 and February 2022.

Several people who are happy to be recognised for their efforts were notably generous with their time and help. Margaret Crick, Michael Crick, Mark Hookham, Sallie Salvidant, Cerys Turner and David Wharton all assisted and advised in different and important ways.

Thanks must also go to the formidable Angela Entwistle and her team, as well as those at Biteback Publishing who were involved in the production of this book. And special thanks to my chief researcher, Miles Goslett.

FAMILY TREE

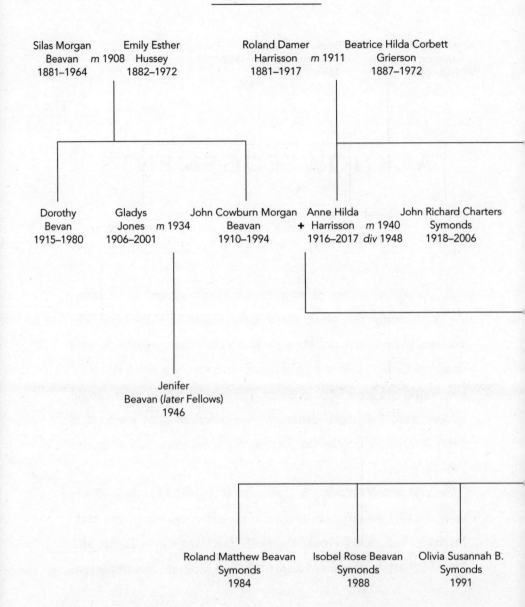

Silas Morgan Beavan 1881–1964 m 1908 Emily Esther Hussey 1882–1972

Roland Damer Harrisson 1881–1917 m 1911 Beatrice Hilda Corbett Grierson 1887–1972

Dorothy Bevan 1915–1980 Gladys Jones 1906–2001 m 1934 John Cowburn Morgan Beavan 1910–1994 + Anne Hilda Harrisson 1916–2017 m 1940 div 1948 John Richard Charters Symonds 1918–2006

Jenifer Beavan (*later* Fellows) 1946

Roland Matthew Beavan Symonds 1984 Isobel Rose Beavan Symonds 1988 Olivia Susannah B. Symonds 1991

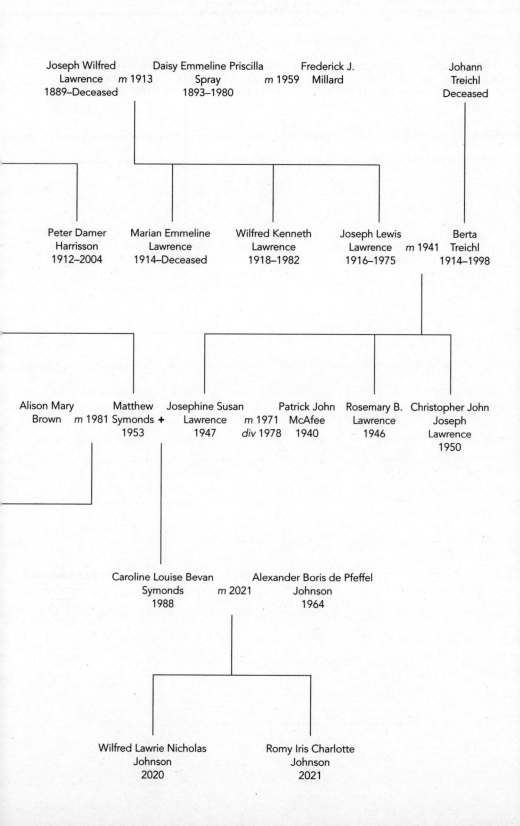

INTRODUCTION

On 24 July 2019, Carrie Symonds entered Downing Street as the first unmarried partner of a Prime Minister in British history. She was thirty-one years old and she was the girlfriend of one of the most polarising politicians to take the highest office in the land, Boris Johnson.

There is no question that becoming the prime ministerial consort, a job for which there is no official description, would be daunting for anybody regardless of their age or the identity of their partner. What might have made the situation for Carrie harder still is that most people who had heard of her in July 2019 probably knew only that she had been named as the young lady who had been accused of being at the centre of Johnson's divorce from his second wife, Marina; or that there had been a domestic dispute involving Johnson at her flat in London the previous month to which the police had been called. To have attracted the attention of the press for such matters before even crossing the threshold of No. 10 must have been unsettling.

What made the circumstances under which Carrie set up home in Downing Street even more unusual was that, thanks to her being a former employee of the Conservative Party and an ex-government special adviser, she was also the first consort of any Prime Minister to be part of what is known as 'the Westminster bubble' – the insular world of Lobby journalists, politicians and aides whose lives are centred around Westminster and Whitehall. Some journalists concluded that her professional background made her a political figure in her own right. Again, this set her apart from previous consorts.

Politics and power are in Carrie's bloodline. As her rather complicated but very colourful family tree shows, her great-grandmother Hilda Harrisson and her grandfather John Beavan also had close friendships with Prime Ministers of their respective eras. Indeed, in the 1970s, Beavan sat as a Labour member of the House of Lords and later went to Brussels as one of Britain's first MEPs. Furthermore, Carrie's father, Matthew Symonds, became a man of public standing in the 1980s when he helped to found a national newspaper, *The Independent*.

Perhaps it should come as no surprise, then, that since 2019, Carrie has come to be thought of by many people in Westminster and beyond as influential herself, especially in the areas of policy and patronage. Power ought to come with accountability. This book addresses a series of events which have dominated Boris Johnson's premiership to date and puts these claims about his now-wife to the test. Often, what I heard about Carrie while working on this project surprised me a great deal. Readers must judge for themselves, however, what her behaviour in a political context says about her relationship with Boris Johnson and what this has meant for the way Britain has been run under him.

Officially, there is no such thing as a First Lady in British politics. This title tends to be associated by most people with the wife of the American President. Yet in the case of Carrie Johnson, as she has been since May 2021, it does not seem entirely out of place that some have ascribed it to her as well. For while it is true that she regards herself as a private individual with no formal role in public life, she has shown a remarkable ambition compared with most, if not all, of her predecessors. This book explores just how far-reaching that ambition has become.

Michael Ashcroft
February 2022

A NOTE ON THE TEXT

I have chosen to refer to Carrie Johnson as 'Carrie' throughout this book. Partly this is to avoid confusion because she changed her surname from Symonds to her married name, Johnson, in May 2021, and much of the text covers her life and career before that date. Using just her Christian name also differentiates her from her husband, Boris Johnson, who is referred to in narrative sections by his surname.

CHAPTER 1

HISTORY REPEATING ITSELF

History has a habit of repeating itself – or, perhaps more accurately, patterns emerge. An assessment of Carrie Johnson's family tree certainly appears to support this conclusion. For although she learned long ago that she came into the world as a result of an extramarital affair, any unease this has brought her should have been ameliorated to some degree by the certainty that she is only following in the footsteps of at least one and potentially two direct relations who were born in similar circumstances: her father, Matthew Symonds; and her grandmother, Anne Symonds. Both rose to success in their chosen field of journalism. Intriguingly, two other forebears, her great-grandmother Hilda Harrisson and her grandfather John Beavan, enjoyed close friendships with Prime Ministers of their day, with Beavan managing to secure a measure of political influence that is beyond the reach of most people. If illegitimacy is in Mrs Johnson's bloodline, therefore, so, arguably, are the arts of journalism and politics, whose ingredients have been so essential to her own career and, ultimately, to her adult life to date. When all of this is considered, maybe the only surprising thing about her now living in Downing Street as the Prime Minister's wife – and arguably the most powerful unelected woman in the United Kingdom after the Queen – is that anybody is surprised by this at all.

The facts behind Carrie Johnson's origins are undeniably absorbing, but they are also somewhat tangled. She was born Caroline Symonds at Queen Mary's Hospital in Roehampton, south-west London, on 17 March 1988. Yet, as will become clear, the surname Symonds, which she inherited from her father and which she used prior to her marriage to Boris Johnson in May 2021, was not rightfully her father's to bestow according to tradition or convention. By extension, neither, arguably, should it have been hers. Unlocking the explanation of how she came to have the Symonds name can only be achieved by first examining the lineage of her father, whose own upbringing was also complicated by marital infidelity, just as Carrie's would be.

Matthew Symonds was born in 1953, the son of Anne Symonds, a divorced BBC broadcaster, and John Beavan, a well-connected left-wing newspaper journalist who was married to another woman, Gladys Jones. Beavan, Carrie's grandfather, was born in the Ardwick district of Manchester in 1910, the product of a staunchly Labour family, and baptised at the Primitive Methodist Chapel there. His father, Silas, who was Carrie's great-grandfather, was born in Hay, in Wales, in 1881 and worked as a miner before becoming a greengrocer in the Manchester area; his mother, Emily, who was Carrie's great-grandmother, was born in 1882 and is said to have been an exceptionally strong character. She rose from humble origins to become a Manchester City councillor, justice of the peace, alderman and women's rights campaigner. She was once in contention to become Manchester's Lord Mayor, but her husband's poor health forced her to decline this opportunity. Her career is commemorated in Openshaw, just outside Manchester, where the street Emily Beavan Close is named in her honour.

John Beavan attended Manchester Grammar School, but his family's finances would not stretch to enabling him to attend a university. He had always wanted to become a journalist anyway and his wish was granted in 1927 when, aged seventeen, he was offered a job as a junior reporter on the *Blackpool Times*. He moved to the *Evening Chronicle* in Manchester in 1928 before taking up a post on the *Manchester Evening News* in 1930. After a decade on that paper, he was hired at the height of the Second World War by the *Evening Standard* in London as an assistant editor on the Londoner's Diary gossip column, the page considered most important by the *Standard*'s owner, the then Minister of Aircraft Production Lord Beaverbrook. Beavan also worked as an *Evening Standard* leader writer. After a short stint as news editor on *The Observer* in 1942, he was made the editor of the *Manchester Evening News* in 1943, a position which came with a seat on the board of its parent company, the Manchester Guardian and Evening News Ltd. In 1946, he began a nine-year spell as London editor of the *Manchester Guardian* (it did not change its name to *The Guardian* until 1959). As the paper was edited and printed in the north of England, the London editor was considered to have a certain cachet. It was during these years in the capital that his affair with Anne Symonds began. It is difficult to be certain when they first became involved with each other. Records show, however, that in October 1951 – that is to say, two years before their son, Matthew, was born – they travelled together as first-class passengers on the Holland America Line's SS *Veendam* from New York to Southampton, having arrived in America together that month via Montreal. Theirs was almost certainly a romance that lasted for some time rather than a casual affair.

The background of Carrie's paternal grandmother, Anne Symonds, was altogether different to that of her grandfather, John Beavan. She was born Anne Harrisson in Liverpool in August 1916 into a more obviously middle-class situation. She was assumed to be the second child of Major Roland Harrisson, a surgeon's son who was killed in action at the Somme in 1917 aged thirty-six, though there are certain reasons why some people believe her father – and therefore Carrie's great-grandfather – to have been somebody else altogether. In 1915, two years before she was widowed, Anne's mother, Hilda, a solicitor's daughter, met the then Liberal Prime Minister Herbert Asquith while playing bridge. Apart from anything else, the fact that this meeting took place at all provides an insight as to the social circles in which the Harrissons moved. Despite Asquith being thirty-six years older than Mrs Harrisson, then in her mid-twenties, they struck up a friendship immediately, corresponding by letter whenever time allowed. So close did they become that rumours persist to this day that Asquith, and not Roland Harrisson, was in fact Anne's father. It's possible this speculation has some basis in fact, for Asquith is known to have had a weakness for young women. For example, just a few years before he met Mrs Harrisson, he had a passionate emotional, and possibly physical, affair with Venetia Stanley, the best friend of his daughter, Violet, when he was sixty years old and Miss Stanley was only twenty-five.

After Asquith left Downing Street in December 1916, he made it his business to keep in touch with Hilda Harrisson. Following the death of her husband – by which time Asquith was Leader of the Opposition – their friendship seems to have intensified. He would have her to stay with him in London and also at his country house in Sutton Courtenay, then part of Berkshire. He is also thought to have supported her financially and, as a young child, Carrie's grandmother, Anne, apparently saw enough of him to refer to him affectionately as 'Uncle Henry' (Henry being his middle name). The hereditary title Earl of Oxford and Asquith was created for Asquith in 1925. When his descendant Raymond, the present and 3rd Earl of Oxford and Asquith, was asked about the nature of the relationship between Herbert Asquith and Hilda Harrisson for the purpose of this book, he said he felt 'quite sure' that they were not linked romantically. His certainty would appear to scotch the idea that Anne was Asquith's daughter and that Asquith was Carrie's great-grandfather.

Perhaps it is true that Herbert Asquith, who was himself widowed in his thirties (he remarried three years later), simply took pity on Hilda Harrisson, meaning their friendship was entirely innocent. And yet it is certainly noteworthy that he wrote several hundred letters to her, right up until 1927, the year before he died. These were published in two volumes in 1933 and 1934 as *Lord Oxford's Letters to a Friend*. In the introduction to that book, Desmond MacCarthy, its editor, observes: 'Like all men of strongly

masculine temperament, women were important in [Asquith's] life
… The lady of the letters stood apart from the main current of his
life. In herself, and also in this respect, she [Hilda Harrisson] was
evidently the intimate woman-friend he needed.'

Asquith described his relationship with Hilda Harrisson in his
own book, *Memories and Reflections*, which was published shortly
after his death. He wrote: 'In June 1915, I formed a new friendship
to which I have since been greatly indebted – my acquaintance
with her ripened after the death of her husband (he was killed in
1917) when in the course of 1918–1919 … we became regular and
intimate correspondents.' While his letters to Hilda Harrisson bear
no definitive trace of the pair having been lovers, and he seems to
have been open – as opposed to secretive – about their friendship,
he was clearly unusually fond of her. For example, on 21 June 1916,
about a year after they had first met and when the First World War
was raging, he wrote to her from Downing Street thanking her for
her latest letters to him and encouraging her to continue writing
to him by saying her missives brought him 'such much-needed
refreshment'. He signed off that letter with the words: 'It is nearly
1 a.m., and I believe I have to go to bed, but I wanted to say "Good-
night" to you. Ever your affectionate, H. H. A.'

No doubt as a result of her mother's closeness to the Prime Minister, Anne Harrisson was apparently interested in politics from
a very early age and became a supporter of the Labour Party as a
young girl. Around that time, she moved with her mother, brother
and grandmother to Boars Hill, a hamlet just outside Oxford, and
was sent aged fifteen to the fee-paying Oxford High School. From
there, in the mid-1930s, she went up to Somerville College, Oxford,

to read Philosophy, Politics and Economics. At Oxford, she was an active member of the Labour Club and socialised with future Labour MPs including Denis Healey and Christopher Mayhew. She also developed an interest in journalism, editing the magazine *Oxford Forward*. After leaving university in 1937, she worked briefly as a researcher for Lord Beaverbrook. Ironically, when Beaverbrook had been an MP more than twenty years previously, he had played a small role in the removal as Prime Minister of Anne's mother's great friend Herbert Asquith in 1916, when he was replaced by Beaverbrook's friend David Lloyd George. By coincidence, Anne's working for Beaverbrook at this time also meant that she knew the press baron shortly before her future lover, John Beavan, worked for him on the *Evening Standard*.

In May 1940, Anne married Richard Symonds, the son of Sir Charles Symonds, an eminent neurologist. The young couple had been at Oxford together. Early in their marriage, in 1942, Richard went to India without Anne as part of Sir Stafford Cripps's unsuccessful mission to gain India's full cooperation in the war effort. After staying in the subcontinent for a prolonged period of time, his relationship with Anne fractured and they were divorced in 1948. That year, Anne was hired as a producer by what was known then as the BBC Overseas Service. Later she became a political correspondent of the BBC World Service, as it was called from 1965, where she worked until the 1970s. Her *Daily Telegraph* obituary, which was published in 2017 when she died aged 100, recorded that her son, Matthew, was 'smuggled into the world'. He was born in his father's home city of Manchester and given the middle name John, presumably after his father, though his surname was not Beavan, as might have been expected. Instead, it was decided that he would take his mother's married name, Symonds. This was despite Anne having long since divorced Richard Symonds and Matthew therefore having no connection to her ex-husband. Richard Symonds died in 2006 aged eighty-seven, having remarried. Carrie is not believed to have ever met him.

John Beavan also had an adopted daughter, Jenifer, who was born in 1946, but it seems that becoming a father to Matthew by a woman other than his wife tamed his spirit to some degree. Aged forty-five, he surprised his colleagues by abandoning newspapers to become the assistant director of the Nuffield Foundation, the educational charitable trust established in 1943 by William Morris, the founder of Morris Motors. This job is said to have supplied him with a generous salary, but in 1960, after five years, journalism came calling again when he was offered the editorship of the *Daily Herald*, by then a struggling left-wing newspaper part-owned by the Trades Union Congress. It changed hands shortly after his arrival and in 1962 its new owner, International Publishing Corporation, transferred him to another title it owned, the *Daily Mirror*, where he was made political editor. This might have seemed like a demotion for a man in his early fifties, but it would have been some consolation to Beavan to know that the *Mirror* was soon selling in excess of 5 million copies per day, an extraordinary achievement not matched by any British newspaper since. Although by the 1970s the *Mirror* had been surpassed as the market leader by *The Sun*, owned since 1969 by Rupert Murdoch, Beavan cemented his own position by twinning his reporting duties with another job, political adviser to the Daily Mirror Group, an appointment he held until 1976.

The fourteen years during which Beavan was the *Mirror*'s political chief, spanning most of the 1960s and half of the 1970s, were among the most fast-moving of the twentieth century in terms of political and societal change. Downing Street's occupants during this period were Harold Macmillan, Alec Douglas-Home, Harold Wilson, Edward Heath and, from March 1974, Harold Wilson again. The importance of newspapers in charting the seismic events of those pre-digital years cannot be overstated. The fact that Beavan interviewed each of these Prime Ministers and knew their staff, and was charged with covering political affairs for the benefit of the *Mirror*'s many millions of readers every day, meant that few journalists were as close to the source of power as he was, particularly when Labour was in government. That he also contributed to some of Wilson's speeches marked him out further. His influence became most obvious in January 1970, five months before that year's general election, when Wilson elevated him to the House of Lords as what might be described as a journalist-peer. Beavan did not sit in the upper chamber under his own surname but chose instead to style himself Lord Ardwick, in recognition of the district of Manchester which he knew so well. This decision might have been considered pretentious, but at the time Wilson did not object to it. In fact, he is said to have commented of this Fleet Street veteran: 'There are lots of people representing the newspaper industry in the Lords. I want John Beavan to represent journalism.'

There is no question that Beavan's career was given fresh impetus after he became a political figure in his own right thanks to his friend and sponsor Harold Wilson. Not only did he take his duties in the Lords seriously, speaking regularly on media matters during debates, but through his closeness to the Prime Minister he also earned himself a new international job. In 1975, Beavan having reached retirement age at the *Mirror*, Wilson next appointed him a Labour Member of the European Parliament, making him one of Britain's first ever MEPs. He stood down in 1979, the first year that MEPs were directly elected, mindful that he was past retirement age and did not have the energy to subject himself to the rigours of an election campaign. As well as both being on the left, he and Anne Symonds further shared a strong enthusiasm for the European political project, a position also held by their son, Matthew, to this day. As shall become clear, this is in contrast to Matthew's daughter, Carrie Johnson.

John Beavan's affair with Anne Symonds did not prevent him and his wife, Gladys, whom he had married in 1934, remaining together until his death from cancer in August 1994. His final years were spent attending the House of Lords and writing lengthy newspaper obituaries of famous friends and key figures he had known from his era of journalism and politics. As well as producing an 8,000-word assessment of Wilson's life, he also charted the careers of Viscount Tonypandy, Lord Cudlipp, Lord Longford, James Callaghan and Michael Foot. Each of these pieces appeared posthumously in the publication with which his son, Matthew, is inextricably linked, *The Independent*.

The life story of Matthew Symonds is no less eventful than that of his parents. He lived with his mother in a shared house at 30 South Eaton Place in Belgravia, which remains one of the smartest areas in London. The Conservative MP Enoch Powell, their neighbour at No. 33, is understood to have become something of a family friend. Matthew was sent to Holland Park School, which was for many years considered the flagship of Britain's progressive post-war educational system. Indeed, it was so popular with those on the left after it was founded in 1958 that it was eventually nick-named the 'Socialist Eton'. This was perhaps inevitable when it is considered that among Symonds's exact contemporaries was, for example, Hilary Benn, the son of the Labour politician Tony Benn.

From Holland Park School, Symonds went up to Balliol College, Oxford (coincidentally the alma mater both of his grandmother Hilda Harrisson's close friend Herbert Asquith and of his daughter's husband, Boris Johnson). Symonds is remembered by some contemporaries who also studied at Oxford in the early 1970s for having drawn attention to himself through his habit of roaring around in a red sports car while wearing dark glasses and leather driving gloves. He was also known for wearing Cuban heels to boost his slight stature. He was considered by some students to be a vain individual who perhaps had a more favourable opinion of himself than did others. Yet he knew some prominent people. As well as his London neighbour Enoch Powell, who made BBC radio programmes with his mother, the Labour Cabinet minister Roy Jenkins also featured in his life. Such connections are said to have strengthened his hand socially, encouraging a university friendship with the future Prime Minister of Pakistan Benazir Bhutto, who called him 'Mattypuffs', and acquaintanceships with others who would go on to make a name for themselves, including the journalist and author Stephen Glover. As an undergraduate, Symonds showed some interest in pursuing his parents into journalism, and he is understood to have been seen occasionally in the offices of *Isis*, the university magazine.

His post-university career got off to a flying start. In 1976, the same year that his father, John Beavan, left the Mirror Group, he was accepted as a graduate trainee on Beavan's old paper, the *Daily Mirror*. Two years later, he moved to the *Financial Times*. Things seemed to stall for him there, however. Part of his job required him to read out share prices on a telephone information line which was run in conjunction with the Post Office. Symonds had a stammer, which proved a major obstacle to his making the four-minute re-cording each hour that was expected of him, so he had to be re-deployed within the syndication department. Stephen Glover, who was by then working as a leader writer on the *Daily Telegraph*, has recalled that Symonds would ring him every six months or so proposing lunch or dinner. 'As time went on, these became for me increasingly gloomy affairs,' Glover has admitted. The reason for their gloominess was that Symonds used these occasions to share with Glover his frustration at his duties, which involved churning out articles on behalf of foreign clients which were not usually even published in the *Financial Times*. Symonds felt unfulfilled. With Glover's help, he landed a new job in 1981 on the *Daily Telegraph* as a junior leader writer specialising in economics. Glover and Symonds had not been close at university, but Glover's assistance would not be forgotten by his new colleague.

Four years later, in June 1985, both men were still working on the *Telegraph*, but the newspaper, then owned by Lord Hartwell, was in serious financial trouble and on the brink of being taken over by the Canadian businessman Conrad Black. One evening that month, Glover was invited by Symonds to meet him at the Kensington house of Andreas Whittam Smith, who was fifteen years their senior and the *Telegraph*'s City editor. It was well known by then that a new mid-market tabloid newspaper called *Today* was soon to be launched by a businessman named Eddy Shah, who was keen to use a range of cost-cutting technological advances to take on the might of the *Daily Mail* and *Daily Express*. The publicity surrounding this enterprise had given Whittam Smith the idea of launching a new quality broadsheet newspaper which he would edit. He had already sounded out Symonds to be his deputy. Though neither he nor Symonds, nor Glover, knew it on the night they met, it would be called *The Independent* and it would begin publishing just over a year later.

Soon after Glover was invited into their circle of trust, the trio became the proposed title's co-founders. After raising millions of pounds of financing, finding premises in City Road in central London, hiring scores of journalists and kitting out the new offices, they saw the paper go on sale for the first time in October 1986. Aged thirty-two, Matthew Symonds became a high-ranking national newspaper executive and also a founding director of Newspaper Publishing Plc, the company which owned *The Independent*. Married with one son, on the face of it he had come a long way since those angst-ridden conversations with Stephen Glover just a few years before.

Yet it was not all plain sailing. Just as he had been regarded by some at Oxford as an outsider, so too, according to certain former colleagues, was he seen as a weak link in the chain of command at *The Independent*. Mark Lawson, who worked in a range of journalistic roles on the paper between 1986 and 1995, recalls:

Andreas Whittam Smith was very tall and Stephen Glover was quite tall, but Matthew was tiny. There's no doubt he had small man syndrome. He wore Cuban heels and pink shirts, which were often commented on by female colleagues and the more bohemian members of staff. I had some sympathy for him because he had such a terrible stammer. It was difficult for him to communicate. For example, I remember in one morning conference he tried to say, 'Bill Clinton has shown grace under pressure,' but he got stuck. It was impossible not to feel for him at those times. So the difficulty of expressing himself perhaps explains why his manner was not brilliant, and he often came across to people as a very unpleasant person. He had no friends in the office and was a loner. His only ally was the columnist Peter Jenkins, who was married to Polly Toynbee. Peter got Matthew involved in the SDP even though Matthew's politics were ferociously right-wing. He was an obsessive free-marketeer. He was the only real right-winger on *The Independent*. Matthew's role was to do the dirty work. So if a column had to be pulled, or someone criticised or sacked, Matthew would do it.

Another journalist who worked closely with Symonds remembers:

Andreas, Stephen and Matthew basically *were* the company, so what they said went. Matthew was around a lot. He would attend the morning editorial conferences, but I was never quite sure what his day-to-day role was. He would make his presence felt, because he was that kind of character. He was very brusque. He was very clever, but in a smartarse and slightly heartless way. He was very sure of himself and contemptuous of other people. He was not a man you warm to. I definitely didn't warm to him. He was very different in character to Stephen and Andreas, who were old-school *Telegraph* Tories in a sort of pre-Thatcher way. Matthew's politics were much more Thatcherite, although notionally he supported the SDP. He also came across as much more rackety than Stephen and Andreas, who were pretty upright characters. He was really interested in the weekly car review. He was interested in cars – he had this air of fast cars, girls, and he was a bit rakish and also a bit insecure.

And another former colleague from *The Independent* says they remember Symonds was also prone to indulging in at least one strange habit during office hours. 'It became a known thing that during morning conference Matthew would sometimes surreptitiously brandish a packet of three condoms,' says this source.

I certainly witnessed it a couple of times and others did as well. I remember they were made by Durex. I think this was his way of telling us he was having sex with someone other than his wife. Maybe it was his way of making up for not being one of the gang. It was as though he was saying, 'I'm having sex that I shouldn't be having.'

While these unflattering assessments of Matthew Symonds's character as a young man may seem to some people to be overly critical, it is clear that *The Independent*'s founding editor, Andreas Whittam Smith, had reservations about him as well. Stephen Glover revealed the source of Whittam Smith's suspicions in his 1992 book *Paper Dreams*, which tells the story of the founding of *The Independent*. In February 1987, just a few months after the paper's launch, Whittam Smith discovered that Symonds had nominated for the vacant job of chief features sub-editor a candidate called Josephine McAfee. She was a qualified barrister who had worked as an editor for the legal book publisher Butterworths and who had done some freelance shifts on *The Independent* as a libel lawyer, but she had little, if any, experience of journalism per se. She was also, to quote the term Matthew Symonds used to describe Mrs McAfee, his 'mistress', though this fact was not widely known at the time of her interview. When Whittam Smith, who was considered to be a man of high morals, was told the truth by another colleague about the married Symonds's relationship with McAfee, a divorcee, he took a dim view. Then, on learning that Symonds had taken his lover to the SDP conference in Harrogate the previous autumn and used his *Independent* expense account to book a double room in a hotel, which had cost £10 more than a single room, he was outraged.

Mark Lawson says that, in hindsight, some who worked on *The Independent* may not have been entirely surprised that Symonds embarked on this extramarital office romance. 'Andreas and Stephen were quasi-clerical in that both were the sons of clergymen,' he says, but there was an awful lot of sex at *The Independent* because it had so many staff who were in their twenties. There was a highly sexualised atmosphere. Younger men who were married with children would have been aware of this bacchanalia. If Matthew received any offers, he might have been flattered by the attention. Looking back, it was probably rather like *The Spectator* was when Boris Johnson was its editor and it became known as the *Sextator*. Many of these liaisons led to marriages, not all of which have lasted. I suppose you could say *The Independent* was a bit Club 18–30.

Whatever Whittam Smith's view of a colleague being unfaithful to his wife, he certainly believed Matthew Symonds's use of his expense account to entertain his paramour to indicate a casual attitude to the use of company money. Not only was he adamant that McAfee should not join the staff of *The Independent*; he also confided in Glover at a secret meeting held at Glover's house one Sunday afternoon his intention to dismiss Symonds for what he considered a breach of company policy. Glover reasoned that £10 was a small sum. He suggested Symonds should be forced to pay it back and reprimanded instead. He also reminded Whittam Smith that the determination and drive shown by Symonds since their initial meeting in June 1985 had been key components of *The Independent*'s successful birth. Without Symonds, Glover told Whittam Smith, the paper would not have existed. He added that sacking him for what he, Glover, called an 'error of judgement' was unthinkable. Nevertheless, a further investigation of Symonds's expenses was ordered immediately, causing a rift between Whittam Smith and Symonds that may have never fully healed.

Tempers did cool briefly, but they were raised again in July 1987 when *Private Eye* got hold of the story of Matthew Symonds and Josephine McAfee. Using information gathered by a mole at *The Independent*, the satirical magazine also revealed how Symonds had taken McAfee to America a few months earlier. To make his humiliation complete, it published details of how he had crashed a BMW motorcycle in the car park of *The Independent*'s offices. The vehicle had been lent to the paper for a road test. Whittam Smith demanded answers from Symonds, no doubt aware that *The Independent*'s chairman, Lord Sieff, the Marks & Spencer heir, might consider such publicity deeply unhelpful to the fledgling company.

Symonds was forced to explain himself. Using his office computer's internal mail system, he wrote to Whittam Smith admitting to the America trip. He said he and Mrs McAfee had stayed at the Algonquin Hotel in New York, which, as mentioned above, was a city to which his own parents had travelled when they were trysting in 1951. Symonds's defence was that the purpose of visiting New York was to end his affair with McAfee. His letter also stated somewhat curiously that the room they had shared at the Algonquin was 'the smallest and cheapest I have had during five stays at the hotel'. He went on: 'In order to make absolutely sure there was no cost to the company, however, I waived my right to fly business class [to America].' He then attempted to explain how he had come to fall off the motorcycle.

When I said that I had not ridden a bike since I was seventeen, I was urged to mount one of the machines ... As I came to a halt, not wishing to negotiate a tight corner, I was taken unawares by the bike's weight and let it drop to the ground.

Having already hacked into the office computer system once, the mole at *The Independent* was only too happy to share the contents of this letter with *Private Eye* as well. It must have been excruciating for Symonds, though some of his colleagues are said to have revelled in his embarrassment.

Matters did not end there. In November 1987, *Private Eye* decided to extract more pain from its victim, publishing a piece titled 'Twenty Things You Never Knew About Matthew Symonds', who, for good measure, was mocked for being 'bouffant haired'. At the top of its list was the revelation that 'Symonds has got himself embroiled in a [Cecil] Parkinson-type situation. Jo McAfee, his former mistress, is now five months pregnant. Since Symonds promised [Andreas Whittam Smith] that he had split up with her well over five months ago, obviously he cannot be the father. Ms McAfee seems to think that he is.' This is the first known public reference to Carrie, and it means that she had the dubious honour of featuring in *Private Eye* while *in utero*, four months before her birth. It would not be the last time she would grace its pages.

The public jeering experienced by Matthew Symonds perhaps failed to acknowledge that others in his life would be hurt by it. His wife, Alison Brown, whom he had married in 1981, and their son, Roland, who had been born in May 1984, spring to mind. On top of any repair work that had to be carried out to his domestic arrangements, Matthew Symonds also had a career to maintain.

Yet, fortunately for him, he weathered the storm's various fronts. Despite Carrie's birth in March 1988, his marriage did not end. Indeed, he and his wife had two more children of their own. Isobel was born in the summer of 1988, just a few months after Carrie, and Olivia followed three years later, in late 1991, meaning that Carrie has three half-siblings.

Matthew Symonds also prospered at *The Independent*, notwithstanding its many financial trials and tribulations, staying on as its deputy editor until 1994, when he left aged forty. At the time of his departure, he owned 544,000 shares in the paper's parent company and is said by former colleagues to have collected pre-tax proceeds of approximately £2 million when the business was restructured and sold in 1995 to a conglomerate comprising Mirror Group Newspapers, Independent News & Media and the Spanish firm PRISA. After leaving *The Independent*, he took a short-lived job as a columnist on the *Sunday Express* before being hired as director of strategy at BBC Worldwide Television, the commercial arm of the BBC. In 1997, he joined *The Economist*, where he served in a variety of editorial roles including as political editor and, between 2010 and 2018, as defence editor. In the latter post he is remembered for having put several journalists' backs up during a specialist press trip to Pakistan in 2016. 'He was rather pompous and very proud of the fact he knew Benazir Bhutto,' remembers one member of the party.

He would tell everyone they'd been friends and would impose himself on every situation, constantly interrupting these Pakistani generals during briefings in order to lecture them on what was really happening in Afghanistan. It got so bad that towards the end, one journalist had to ask him if he would please just let the generals talk a bit.

In 2018, he left *The Economist*, having been appointed executive director of the Larry Ellison Foundation, the eponymous charity set up by the American technology billionaire.

Regardless of his own eventual successes, however, the rather extraordinary fact is that, as a young man in the 1980s, Matthew Symonds trod the very same path that his father, John Beavan, found himself on in the 1950s. Both were successful journalists who were married with one child at the time they embarked on an affair with a divorced woman who then gave birth out of wedlock to their second child. In Carrie's case, this left her, like Matthew Symonds before her, to be brought up as the only child in a single-parent household. What is perhaps just as remarkable in terms of history repeating itself is that in 2018 Carrie, like her mother more than thirty years before her, would also strike up an affair with a married father, Boris Johnson, albeit she was not herself a divorcee.

Carrie's mother, Josephine, came from a far more traditional family compared with that of Matthew Symonds. She was born Josephine Lawrence at Newark in Nottinghamshire in 1947. She had an elder sister, Rosemary, and a younger brother, Christopher. Her father, Carrie's maternal grandfather, was Dr Joseph Lawrence, who was known by his middle name, Lewis. He was born in Pontypool in 1916, the son of a stoker, Joseph Wilfred Lawrence, who was Carrie's great-grandfather, and a domestic servant, Daisy Spray, Carrie's great-grandmother. Shrugging off the constraints of his upbringing, Lewis Lawrence was bright enough to enrol as a medical student at King's College, London, in 1934. He qualified in 1940 and served as a squadron leader in the RAF Medical Brigade during the Second World War.

In September 1941, he married Berta Treichl, Carrie's maternal grandmother, at the Brompton Oratory, the Roman Catholic church in Knightsbridge. Their marriage was unusual for two reasons. First, Miss Treichl had been born at Kufstein in western Austria in 1914, where her father is thought to have worked as a railway official. As Austria had been annexed by Adolf Hitler in 1938, and was therefore officially part of Nazi Germany, this meant that, technically, Dr Lawrence married a German national in the midst of the Second World War. At the outbreak of war, in 1939, Miss Treichl had been forced to take part in a tribunal at which her status as a security risk was assessed. Her desire to stay in Britain was sanctioned and she was issued with an Enemy Alien Exemption from Internment form. This helps to explain the second reason her marriage might have been considered unconventional for the time. This form states that she worked as a domestic servant at Battramsley House in the village of Boldre in Hampshire, an estate then owned by a member of the Barings banking family. As middle-class pillars of the community, doctors like Lewis Lawrence did not tend to marry cooks, as Miss Treichl was. Their union is believed to have been successful, however. After the war, Lewis became a gynaecological surgeon and worked in different parts of the country until his death aged fifty-nine in 1975, while Berta worked as a receptionist.

Carrie's mother, Josephine, was brought up as a Roman Catholic and in 1971, in her early twenties, she married Patrick McAfee, a banker, at the Church of the Immaculate Conception in Mayfair, central London. On their marriage certificate, her occupation is listed as 'bank official'. They divorced in 1978 and Patrick McAfee remarried the following year. After this, Josephine trained in the law. According to the Bar Council, she was called to the Bar in February 1987 as a member of Lincoln's Inn. The Bar Council's records suggest that she was never in practice, however, and was not a member of any chambers. She was forty years old at the time of Carrie's birth in 1988, six years Matthew Symonds's senior.

Josephine and Carrie lived together in a semi-detached three-bedroom Victorian house just off the Upper Richmond Road in East Sheen, an affluent but unshowy south-west London suburb. At about 1,100 sq. ft and with a 40 ft garden, it was not a big property, but it was well located, being close to the pleasures of Richmond Park. This is the area where Carrie's childhood was spent and where her mother still lives. When Carrie's birth certificate was registered by Josephine, it appears there was some misunderstanding about one of her daughter's two middle names. The first of these is listed on the certificate as 'Louise' but her second middle name, 'Bevan', seems to be a misspelled version of the surname of Matthew's father, John Beavan. This can be deduced because each of Matthew's other three children also have 'Beavan' – spelled correctly – as one of their middle names. Unless this was intentional, under the circumstances it is unfortunate to note that Carrie's 'Bevan' is slightly different. In a way, however, this sense of otherness could be considered a reflection of the hard truth that her life was blessed with fewer familial relationships than it might have been. Indeed, despite her living in close proximity to some of her relatives when growing up, there is little evidence of her having had any meaningful contact with many of them.

At the time of Carrie's birth in 1988, Matthew Symonds lived in Twickenham, about three miles down the road from East Sheen. Soon after, he moved with his wife and family to a significantly bigger house, also in Twickenham, which he sold in 2021 for a little more than £5 million. In a 1996 newspaper interview, Andreas Whittam Smith, who can be said to have known Symonds as well as anybody in the 1980s and 1990s, praised him as 'highly intelligent' and somebody who is 'capable of big organisational feats'. Having presumably put aside his earlier reservations about Symonds, he also spoke of their shared views on business, economics and policy, a credo he called 'economic liberalism'. Yet he was prepared to acknowledge that some people believed there was another side to his former colleague. 'Matthew's reputation has been of a rather harsh, arrogant, rigid person, and I've always been sorry about that, because it's not the real person, it's merely a mannerism,' he said. Perceptions of an individual's true character are rarely unanimous, and this is certainly the case of Matthew Symonds. Oliver Haiste, a former boyfriend of Carrie who dated her on and off between 2007 and 2012, says that even though her father lived within easy reach of East Sheen, he was a fairly distant figure in her life during her childhood. 'Carrie was kept at bay, largely because Matthew's wife didn't want the reminder of his affair,' says Haiste.

I think it was hard for her. She felt almost like the adjunct to [Matthew's] main family. She did mention that. I got the impression he had his family, he would do his basic duty [for Carrie], but that was it. Carrie wasn't very keen on her father. He'd turn up from time to time, but Carrie was not always available to see him.

Of the three grandparents who were still alive at the time of Carrie's birth, her maternal grandmother, Berta Lawrence, through whom Carrie is one-quarter Austrian, is believed to have lived in London until she died in 1998, when Carrie was ten, in the Nazareth House nursing home in Isleworth. Unusually, there is no trace of Mrs Lawrence having left a will. Carrie's paternal grandfather, John Beavan, lived in Barnes, about two miles from East Sheen, but a source close to Carrie's family says that Beavan had 'almost nothing' to do with Carrie before he died when she was six years old. In his will, he left an estate with a gross value of just over £200,000. His grandchildren – including Carrie – were given £1,000 each. The principal beneficiary was his wife, Gladys, who died in 2011. The rest of his estate went to his daughter, Jenifer Fellows, who is Matthew Symonds's half-sister and therefore, technically, Carrie's aunt. Matthew was not mentioned in the will. Mrs Fellows, a retired teacher, has a husband and two daughters. By coincidence, she also lived in East Sheen throughout Carrie's childhood, in a house which was only about two minutes' walk from Carrie's front door. Oddly, however, a well-placed source says that she has never met Carrie or her mother, though she did meet her father's lover – and Carrie's paternal grandmother – Anne Symonds.

Anne Symonds was also remembered in John Beavan's will, receiving a gift of £1,000. Latterly, she lived in Oxfordshire and died in a nursing home in Woking. She left an estate with a gross value of £1.2 million. Each of her four grandchildren, including Carrie, was given £3,000, but the bulk of her legacy was left to her son, Matthew. Her will stipulated that the three children Matthew had had by his wife, Alison, could share in any residue of her estate in certain circumstances. For reasons best known to Anne Symonds, Matthew's other daughter, Carrie, was excluded from this conditional bequest.

CHAPTER 2

LOW PROFILE

Although Carrie had what might be described as a fairly mud-dled start in life, she was extremely fortunate in one sense. Whereas her father, Matthew Symonds, was sent to a state school, he agreed that his four children would be educated privately at his expense. Given that they lived in different houses and had different mothers, it was probably inevitable that Carrie would attend a different school from her three half-siblings, yet there was no distinction between the reputations of these establishments. Symonds, newly wealthy following his seven-figure windfall from *The Independent*, was easily able to foot the bill for all of his offspring to receive the highest standard of teaching available in London. Carrie entered this privileged environment when she was of primary school age and remained in it all the way through to the time she took her A-Levels aged eighteen.

The first private school she is known to have attended was Bute House Preparatory School for Girls in Hammersmith. As it was situated on the other side of the River Thames from her home, and getting to it therefore involved a journey by car or on public transport, it would not have been the automatic choice of every parent who lived in East Sheen. Other fee-paying schools were closer. When Carrie arrived there in the 1990s, however, it was widely considered to be the best academic prep school for girls in west London, showing that at least one of her parents had high hopes for her. Despite Bute House's metropolitan location, it occupies a pleasant site in Luxemburg Gardens, a residential road of handsome Victorian terraced houses close to Brook Green. It was founded in 1958 under the trusteeship of the Worshipful Company of Mercers, the premier livery company of the City of London, and has always had good facilities and access to generous grounds. All of this came at a cost. Annual fees were about £4,500 when she joined the school and had risen to approximately £6,500 by the time she left aged eleven in the summer of 1999.

Bute House was a popular choice among middle-class parents who worked in politics, the media and the arts. With approximately 300 pupils aged from four to eleven, places were in demand as waiting lists were long. The headmistress throughout Carrie's early school career was Sallie Salvidant, who commuted to London each week from her home in north Devon. She says she believes that Carrie started there aged seven in 1995. 'We called her Caroline at school,' she remembers. 'She was never Carrie, always Caroline. I think she came in at the seven-plus stage when the year group size expanded.' Being accepted by Bute House was by no means easy, with about 120 children vying for only twenty-five or thirty places. According to Mrs Salvidant, girls who were offered a place at seven had to be bright, engaging and have an enquiring mind. 'She would have been in a very competitive situation aged seven doing reading comprehension, maths and various other activities,' she says. 'Then she would have had an interview with one of the staff or with me. Then we would have gone around the school together. So she obviously was bright and confident enough to get through that competitive situation.'

Mrs Salvidant says that, despite Bute House being selective from the age of seven, it operated a system which was designed to be informal, with no streaming or tests. Instead of work being traditionally marked by teachers, they marked by 'remark', verbally or in writing. Some parents may have felt this arrangement was rather unusual, but it appears to have been extremely effective. 'We had a different ethos from other London prep schools,' Mrs Salvidant recalls.

We didn't have grades or exams apart from spelling and tables tests. There was a unique non-competitive academic ethos. Once the children were accepted, they were running their own best race rather than being in competition. The first intake by ballot at the age of four was totally mixed ability and siblings were always given preference. We had children with special needs, we had children of every ability who had siblings in the school. We never asked them to leave. They stayed on. At seven when there was an assessment, we weren't just looking for academic ability but also for those with a curiosity and an innate intelligence who would get the best from what we had to offer. We didn't always offer to a child with beautiful handwriting or perfect spelling. Creativity was important, too. It was a very unusual prep school. We didn't even do mock exams and we never had form orders, so nobody could say they were top or bottom of a form or subject. That may have been why we were so popular. It was not a pushy school and yet it probably had some of the best results in London.

The school had a well-equipped science laboratory and an unusually large library, but there was much emphasis on extracurricular activities as well. Art and drama were taken seriously as subjects and there were chess, philosophy and debating societies. Music lessons were held during school hours and there were choirs and two orchestras. There were also fortnightly school council meetings so that democratic discussions could take place about issues raised by pupils, such as litter-picking or choosing a charity to support, thereby encouraging responsibility among pupils. And each year, a group of Year 6 girls would take part in a field trip to the area of Devon where Mrs Salvidant lived. With such a range of opportunities available in a climate that was both liberal and forward-looking and yet firm, perhaps it is no wonder that some of the girls Bute House produced from that era have gone on to achieve success and recognition. Among those who were in the school at the same time as Carrie were the writer and actress Phoebe Waller-Bridge, who was a couple of years ahead of her; the model Suki Waterhouse, who was three years below her; and the actress Imogen Poots, who was in the year below her. 'We weren't affiliated to St Paul's Girls' School, though people assumed we were because we were on the same site,' adds Mrs Salvidant. 'But we shared grounds with St Paul's, so we had immediate access to playing fields, tennis courts and a swimming pool.'

Mrs Salvidant says she made extensive enquiries among twenty or so of her former colleagues to see if any of them had a distinct memory of Carrie. None did, however. 'She was a good, hard-working, sensible little girl,' says Mrs Salvidant,

> but nobody can remember her being particularly musical or arty. I can remember the girls who were hauled up in front of me for being naughty, and she was not one of those. I remember the children who perhaps were brilliant artists or musicians or sports stars, but she didn't obviously stand out. I do remember her mother was very supportive of the school and always thanked us for what we did. She would come to parents' evenings regularly. We didn't see so much of her father, but I know he was supportive of her. There didn't seem to be any conflict [between her parents]. Carrie's mother was an active and supportive parent who was involved, pleasant and easy to deal with.

Large numbers of Bute House's alumnae were bright enough to go on to the aforementioned St Paul's Girls' School, one of London's top independent senior schools. Not far behind it in the academic pecking order was another well-known girls' school, also based in Hammersmith, called the Godolphin and Latymer School. Situated in Iffley Road, close to Hammersmith Tube Station, the more handsome of its buildings date from the nineteenth century, when it was founded as a boys' boarding school before being re-established as a girls' school in 1905. In the late 1990s it was regarded as a fairly prestigious place whose recently departed old girls – known as Old Dolphins – included the actress Kate Beckinsale, the future MEP Annunziata Rees-Mogg and the singer Sophie Ellis-Bextor.

Reflecting its status, Lady Patten, the wife of Sir Chris Patten, as he was then styled, was appointed the chair of the governors in 2000. It was to this establishment that Carrie applied. Again, she appears to have flourished in the highly competitive environment of tests and friendly interrogations that had to be negotiated before being accepted by such an institution. Having passed an entrance examination, she was required to attend two formal interviews. Only then was her name one of the 100 chosen from the list of 500 applicants. She joined the school in September 1999.

Margaret Rudland was the headmistress throughout Carrie's seven years at Godolphin and Latymer. 'It was a voluntary aided grammar school under the 1944 Education Act and returned to independence in 1977,' Miss Rudland explains. 'By the time Caroline came it was a well-established independent school. She came into the school by competitive entry, she did entrance tests and interviews as everybody did, and she was much in line with everybody who came to the school.' With about 700 pupils spread across seven years, the student body was certainly more cosmopolitan than she would have been used to at her smaller prep school, yet despite the obvious change in tempo in the classroom, Miss Rudland did her best to ensure no girls found it an intimidating place. 'I would say the school was academically rigorous,' she recalls.

There were some girls in the school who were outstandingly academic. It had been a very prestigious grammar school and it kept that reputation. It was a well-organised school, but essentially I think it was a friendly school, with good and warm relationships between the staff and the pupils. I only had to watch the faces of the girls coming in in the morning. They all seemed happy to come to school, probably to see their friends, but I think everybody said it was a friendly school.

Making a contribution outside of the classroom was actively encouraged. 'We expected girls would do their work but would also take part in extracurricular activities,' notes Miss Rudland.

I'd say the school was strong in music, sport and drama. Drama was very popular and hugely important to the girls. When Caroline was there, we didn't have much of a performance space … but she did take part in Drama. Facilities in Iffley Road were not extensive. There was one sports field big enough for hockey and in the summer was transformed into nine tennis courts. There were additional hard courts for netball and hard tap tennis. We started using off-site facilities such as rowing on the river and using the Lyric Theatre in Hammersmith for large productions.

Unusually, pupils had to study food and nutrition during their first three years in the school, with a mandatory cookery lesson every other week and an annual *MasterChef*-style competition. *The Godolphin and Latymer School Magazine 2000–2001* confirms that Carrie made it to the final of her year's *MasterChef* when she was in the lower fourth, aged twelve, but her penne Florentine was not deemed to be the tastiest dish on offer by the judges, listed as Mrs Foster and Mrs Watson, who considered the chicken curry made by Carrie's contemporary Radhika Patel to be more delicious. Although there was no school theatre on the premises in Carrie's day, sixth form girls did oversee and organise plays acted in by younger girls. In the same year that Carrie's culinary skills took her to the *MasterChef* final, her form was involved in a production of *The Witches* by Roald Dahl. A brief account in the school magazine observed: 'Acting was excellent all round, but special mention must go to Caroline Symonds, who can only be described as a natural frog.' A grainy photograph of her in an amphibian costume accompanied this glowing notice.

As Carrie became more senior, reports of her progress in the school magazine became fewer and further between. At the age of thirteen, she did have a joint byline on a piece about a history trip to Ypres to visit war graves and battlefields. Yet despite the comprehensively logged news of debating competitions, plays and concerts, sporting fixtures, art shows, charity drives and excursions abroad – together with examples of pupils' poetry and creative writing, which occupied the pages of subsequent editions of the magazine over the next five years – her name featured only twice more. In her final year, her A-Level Drama group's exam performances of *An Adaptation of A Doll's House* and *An Adaptation of The Crucible* were praised by her teacher Sarah Adams for being 'imaginatively staged'. She was also one of twenty-three girls in her year to be given a leaving prize, which, according to one contemporary, was 'basically a consolation prize' for those pupils who had not won one of the various special academic or music awards. Furthermore, all available records suggest she did not hold any position of responsibility in the school. Certainly, she was not made head girl; nor was she one of the head girl's five deputies. And if she was a member of any competitive sports teams, the editors of the school magazine failed to register it.

Some will be surprised at this apparent lack of visibility in a figure such as Carrie, whose drive as an adult has never been in doubt, but one acquaintance says: 'I know a few people who were at school with her. The impression they gave me is she wasn't particularly well known at school. You might have thought she'd have been a mover and shaker, but apparently she wasn't.' And Margaret Rudland says that, casting her mind back more than fifteen years, she does not remember her former charge as having been a big personality either. On the other hand, she was not a pupil who required any special consideration. 'I can remember her at school, but she wasn't somebody who came to my attention … She hadn't got academic issues or disciplinary issues or pastoral issues. So she wasn't somebody coming to my door all the time,' Miss Rudland says. 'I would have said she was quite low-profile. She went through school pretty seamlessly from beginning to end.' When asked if there are girls who were in her year who are easier to recall today, Miss Rudland replies: 'There are,' adding: 'in the sense that I used to go and watch them at sport, concerts and plays. She didn't stand out. I do remember her being involved in Drama.' Whether this absence of prominence was of any concern to her single-minded father, who was paying fees of about £11,000 a year by the time Carrie left the school, is not known. Was her status as a child from a single-parent household at all unusual? Miss Rudland thinks not. 'I remember very clearly that when I became head in 1986, most girls seemed to be living with two parents,' she says. 'As the years went on, that dwindled, sadly. Carrie would not have felt particularly different. There would have been others in her form [from single-parent households], others among her friends.'

One exact contemporary of Carrie who did not wish to be identified publicly echoed much of what their former headmistress had to say. She prefaced her assessment of Carrie's character by explaining that they were not notably close during their schooldays. 'In my whole seven years with her, being part of a relatively small year of about 110 girls, we were never particularly good friends,' she says. 'I was quite shy at school, though, so that may have been my fault.' Yet this person's memories of Carrie are sufficiently strong that she was prepared to reflect objectively upon those insights that she did retain. 'She wasn't obviously rebellious,' remembers this former classmate.

Our year was generally very well behaved, so there weren't many issues with drugs or smoking. I remember her being ambitious and hard-working. She wasn't necessarily the brightest in the year, but I'm pretty sure she would've been in the first or second set for everything. I wouldn't say she had a huge number of friends, but she did have a small, close group. I don't know whether she thought she was better than everyone else – a few people definitely didn't like her as they thought she was snobby and a social climber. Although I never experienced this at first hand, I can confirm that this was her reputation. I don't think she was particularly sporty. At least, she didn't play in the main school teams. She was definitely part of the thespian crowd and she was interested in animal rights and environmental issues, although, having said that, there was a Green Society that held weekly lunch break meetings and I don't remember her ever being part of it. She wasn't part of the committee that ran it. Maybe it was because it was a bit uncool.

She adds: 'Carrie wasn't loud and was quite a private person.'

Several other exact contemporaries have said they just remember her as a 'sweet' girl, one of whose closest friends was Anna Pinder, the daughter of a History teacher at Godolphin and Latymer. Pinder and Carrie remain on very good terms today. Another close friend was Clare Williams. It is fair to say that among her other classmates were the offspring of some well-heeled and prominent families. Ownership of an estate in Scotland was not unheard of, for example; nor was having a father who was a frontbench MP or a senior figure in the City or the law. Wealth and success were not foreign currencies to a proportion of the girls, in other words. With this in mind, Carrie's ex-boyfriend Oliver Haiste, who began a relationship with her when she was nineteen, shortly after she left school, has identified a few possible explanations as to why she might not have been as popular as some of her other classmates during her senior school career. 'By London standards, Carrie felt hers was a fairly modest upbringing,' says Haiste. 'She and her mother lived in a perfectly nice house in a nice area, but Carrie always said compared to other girls she felt her life was modest.' Any sense of social or financial inferiority she might have felt was not helped by an illness which disrupted her school attendance record and therefore her social life. Haiste adds:

There was a period at school when I think she felt she'd been slightly sidelined by her friends. One of the reasons she was very close to Clare Williams is that she stuck by her. Some people are naturally shy and they become extroverts in later life by necessity, even if they're not naturally that way inclined. You get this a lot with stand-up comedians, for example. Offstage, they're quiet and surprisingly understated. And that's her. I think she is quite shy. I'd say she almost contrived to be extrovert [later in life].

If this alleged diffidence did indeed show itself at school, it was not always evident during the holidays, when she was capable of bursts of exuberance. For example, one Christmas Day when she was aged twelve or thirteen was spent at the London home of Florence Lawes, whom she describes as her oldest friend, or 'womb mate', because their mothers met in hospital shortly before they gave birth to their daughters in March 1988. After their Christmas lunch, the two girls disappeared to a nearby churchyard to drink bottles of an alcopop called WKD. On the way back to Florence's house, no doubt spurred on by a small amount of liquor, 'they played a game which involved flashing every man over fifty who was walking down the street', according to Frances Charles, another friend who is familiar with the story. This was surely reflective of a certain liveliness in Carrie, who is reckoned to have been the instigator of the prank.

Such behaviour might have shocked her mother, had she known about it. As Oliver Haiste comments, Josephine McAfee is a 'pious' woman and regular churchgoer who raised her daughter in the Roman Catholic faith. Carrie took her First Holy Communion at St Winefride's Church in Kew, and as a girl is remembered by other parishioners for having attended mass there on Saturday evenings with her mother. There is no doubt she was brought up to behave with decorum, but the question of how lonely she was, and what effect this might have had on her personality, is hard to avoid. '[In effect] Carrie had no grandparents, siblings or father,' says Haiste.

> Her life was very mother-centric. And there was no male figure in Josephine's life after Carrie arrived, as I understand it. She'd been married and divorced and that was that. She retired very early, aged about forty or forty-one. She was active in terms of going out, but I don't think she had a part-time job or anything.

This perceived sense of unwanted isolation might even have bred some bitterness. 'Josephine always seemed very dismissive of Matthew,' adds Haiste.

> Bearing in mind he is a journalist, I remember she once said he couldn't even distinguish the spelling between 'counsellor' and 'councillor'. She was always bringing up little things like that. Carrie talked lots about how hurtful she found it that her father was absent. She'd say her father was completely absent from her life and she'd say her mother was cold. She did love her mother a lot, there's no denying that. She was very close to her mother, but her mother appeared quite cold in terms of being affectionate. It left its mark.

According to one source, Carrie rarely if ever visited her father at his house in Twickenham, though he would visit her in East

Sheen, often on a Thursday or Friday evening. Even if there is a view that Matthew Symonds did not make a very heavy emotional investment in their lives, however, it is thought that he remained an essential figure in other ways. Josephine was not a rich woman, she did not work, and therefore Matthew's financial contribution to their household is thought by necessity to have gone above and beyond the mere payment of Carrie's school fees. While it is quite natural for an absent middle-class professional father to provide for his child in all sorts of ways, the arrangement was probably not considered ideal by any party concerned.

Light relief was to be found for Carrie and her mother elsewhere, notably in Dorset, where Josephine has co-owned a holiday home near the seaside town of Swanage for many years, allowing Carrie to spend some of her childhood there. Indeed, she has continued to spend time there as an adult and is known to favour lengthy coastal walks, covering up to twenty miles at a time.

Godolphin and Latymer had very few formal social events with other schools, though it did sometimes double up with the nearby Latymer Upper School, most of whose pupils are boys, for outings and trips. The two schools also supplied children for a joint orchestra and for some plays. The opposite sex did not figure particularly highly on Carrie's agenda during her time at school, though. Indeed, according to her friend Frances Charles, Carrie did not kiss a boy until she was sixteen years old.

Academic matters were never far from any girl's mind at Godolphin and Latymer. During Carrie's final years in the school, more than 88 per cent of pupils achieved A*s or As in their GCSEs and 89 per cent achieved As and Bs at A-Level. About 15 per cent of pupils went on to Oxford or Cambridge and many girls aimed for careers in medicine. Such expectations could be a burden for those who were not considered to be the cream of the crop. If Carrie was not thought of straight away by the staff of Godolphin and Latymer as Oxbridge material, she was well suited to the general style of tuition available in the sixth form courtesy of smaller class sizes and more discussion with teachers. The fact that sixth formers did not have to wear a school uniform and had their own common room also helped to create an atmosphere that was slightly less rigid than some comparable schools. Teaching staff spent whatever time was required on supporting those whose confidence had dipped for any reason.

As acting was one of her principal interests as a child (she is said by Oliver Haiste to have mastered the notoriously tricky art of being able to shed tears on cue) it was perhaps unsurprising that in the spring of 2006, as her school career came to an end, she apparently decided to put herself through the ultimate test by auditioning for a role in the high-profile film *Atonement*, starring Keira Knightley. This adaptation of Ian McEwan's novel, spanning the 1930s to the 1990s, centres on the character of Briony Tallis, who comes from a wealthy English family and, aged thirteen, makes an allegation about a young man which has devastating consequences. In the film, Knightley plays Cecilia Tallis, Briony's elder sister. Hundreds of girls from all over Britain tried out for two other parts – Briony aged thirteen and Briony aged eighteen. Among them, allegedly, was Carrie, who would have been aware that shooting was due to begin in late June – the very time that she was due to complete her A-Levels in English Literature, Drama and History of Art.

The Irish actress Saoirse Ronan, then twelve years old, eventually won the part of Briony aged thirteen; and Romola Garai, aged twenty-three, was chosen to play Briony aged eighteen. Although the film's casting director, Jina Jay, says she has no recollection of Carrie's audition, Oliver Haiste, who began dating her the following year, says: 'Carrie claimed she had gone for the [role played by] Saoirse Ronan.' Carrie certainly appeared fresh-faced as an eighteen-year-old, but given her age it seems just as likely that she in fact auditioned for the part of Briony aged eighteen. Whichever role she perhaps went for, this early failure is said to have been the cause of much regret to her as she prepared to leave school. 'She made the last few [candidates for the role],' says Haiste.

> She said she was quite disappointed. She didn't go for other parts after that. I don't know why. Maybe she realised it was always going to be that type of struggle. I think her mother would have been keen on her becoming an actress. She used to go to the theatre herself quite a lot so I think she would have supported her.

Carrie had every reason to feel disheartened. Not only was *Atonement* a major critical and commercial success around the world when it was released in 2007, but Ronan was nominated for an Oscar in the Best Actress in a Supporting Role category, setting her on the road to stardom. Garai's career, too, benefited enormously from her association with the film.

Although Carrie is not remembered by her peers for having been at the very top of the academic tree at school, she was certainly capable. High-ranking universities like Bristol, Durham, Edinburgh,

Exeter, UCL and Imperial were the most popular choices for pupils of her ability. When her A-Level results came through and she was found to have secured a string of A grades, she took up an offer made by the University of Warwick to read Theatre Studies. This was, perhaps, a curious choice given the recent anguish caused by her failure to land a part in *Atonement*. Without taking a year off, however, she headed to Warwick's campus on the outskirts of Coventry in September 2006 to begin the next phase of her life.

CHAPTER 3

NEAR MISS

Some who move in academic circles can still be rather sniffy about Britain's newer universities, while others are equally scornful of certain undergraduate arts degrees. Yet when Carrie enrolled at the University of Warwick in the autumn of 2006, the compilers of the *Sunday Times University Guide* could not have been more enthusiastic about both her chosen institution, which was founded in 1965, and the course she had signed up to, Theatre Studies. Indeed, in the newspaper's opinion, Warwick had by then earned a reputation as one of the country's most well thought of seats of learning. 'In barely 40 years, Warwick has established itself as a leading alternative to Oxford and Cambridge,' the guide's authors declared. 'It recruits some of the brightest students who are taught by staff often working at the cutting edge of their subjects.' They rated Warwick's Theatre Studies offering 'excellent'. And they concluded that the university, which had just formed a partnership with the Royal Shakespeare Company and secured £4.5 million of funding to establish a centre for theatre performance, was the sixth best in the UK overall.

As a member of the Russell Group, the self-selected association of twenty-four top British institutions akin to America's Ivy League, Warwick was slightly unusual in taking Theatre Studies as seriously as it did. The course was not about acting per se; nor was it targeted solely at those who wished to make acting their profession, even if some Theatre Studies graduates have gone on to make a living by working in theatre, television or film. Instead, students had to have achieved three decent A-Level results and be prepared to knuckle down to three years' study, which was more scholastic than many might assume. The number of single honours Theatre Studies undergraduates was fairly low, at about forty per year, meaning they all tended to know each other well.

According to one former student who was a contemporary of Carrie's, Theatre Studies had been on Warwick's curriculum for decades, but it was felt by some staff that standards had slipped by the turn of the decade, five or six years before Carrie's arrival. The university authorities decided that the only way the course could be saved was to invest in it. New tutors were recruited from other institutions and new premises opened in Milburn House, now the base for several of Warwick's Faculty of Arts subjects. When Carrie was an undergraduate, the course is said to have consisted of learning about traditional theatre history such as Restoration drama and Ancient Greek plays. Some more radical teaching was also introduced which focused on urban theatre and modules such as Community Theatre Practice; Theatre and National Identity; and Women in the Theatre. Still, without intending to sound dismissive of her, a close friend of Carrie's who knew her well when she was at university says: 'Carrie's very socially intelligent. She's very good academically in terms of exam achievements. But she herself knew that by doing Theatre Studies at Warwick she wasn't reading astrophysics at Cambridge.'

Her first three terms at Warwick coincided with the last period of the Tony Blair era, and life for university students at that time was relatively straightforward. Tuition fees had been introduced, but they were capped at £3,000 per year, as opposed to almost £10,000 per year now. The global financial crisis had not yet erupted. And British politics was arguably more clearly defined insofar as the divisions caused by such issues as the Brexit referendum, or the complications wrought by social media platforms, were still a decade away. If any 'culture wars' were being fought in 2006, the battles were certainly less aggressive and the stakes for the losers lower than they are in the 2020s. Perhaps above all else, the idea of a global pandemic curtailing anybody's freedom in those days was nothing more than a glint in the eye of a Hollywood scriptwriter. The first decade of the twenty-first century was certainly an easier time in which to be a carefree undergraduate aged eighteen.

Carrie was one of about 6,000 students who lived on the university campus, which has an arts centre with a 1,500-seat concert hall, a couple of theatres, a cinema and an art gallery. For most new arrivals in her day, the social scene was driven by the student union, ultimately contributing to a feeling among some freshers that the university could be quite an insular place once the initial excitement of living away from home had worn off. When students did venture off Warwick's campus, they tended to spend little time in the nearest city, Coventry, preferring to frequent the restaurants, pubs and nightclubs of Leamington Spa instead. Not only is

Leamington Spa closer to the campus; it is generally considered to be safer and more attractive. Warwick being only about 100 miles from London did mean that Carrie could return to her mother's house in East Sheen as often as she wished.

She soon got into the swing of campus life, striking up new friendships which supplanted those that had been forged at school and becoming a well-known fixture on the social scene. At one early fancy-dress party she captured attention by putting on a short skirt and tying her long hair into pigtails to achieve the look of the American singer Britney Spears, who had starred in a music video dressed as a schoolgirl a few years previously. It was not unusual for joints, pills and powders to be offered at such gatherings. 'Party drugs were available at Warwick just as they would be at any university,' recalls one contemporary. 'I wouldn't say that the crowd Carrie ran with were doing this sort of thing every day of the week, though.'

Outside of the lecture theatre, most students spend their first year at university revelling in their new-found freedom, lapping up every experience on offer and getting to grips with the fact that they are now in charge of their own affairs and have to accept some responsibility for themselves. In all of this, Carrie was no different to any of her peers. Twelve years after graduating from Warwick, she lists on her LinkedIn profile the activities and societies she enjoyed there as 'Lacrosse, Running, Acting, Debating, Events Planning, Art History, Creative and Critical Writing, Fundraising, Arts Marketing, British Politics, International Development'. Groups and societies at universities come and go, and it would be hard to identify the precise level of her input in all of these pursuits more than a decade later. Yet what is clear is that she is not remembered for having taken part in some of these activities in a mainstream sense. For example, she was not a prominent figure in student politics or in the student union. Nor is she believed to have become heavily involved in student journalism. Indeed, having checked the issues of the student newspaper, *The Boar*, which were published during the three years she was at Warwick, her name was never mentioned in it. She did, however, play lacrosse and do some acting in addition to concentrating on her studies.

In July 2007, the harmonious manner in which her life had been proceeding up until that point was interrupted by an extremely unsettling experience whose relevance was not obvious to her, or to anybody else, straight away. One night during the long summer vacation, she went out with a couple of friends in London. Their last stop was a club on the King's Road in Chelsea. Among the group was Oliver Haiste, whom she had met a few times before but had not yet begun to date. Having parted ways in the early hours, she waited alone for a night bus to take her home to East Sheen. Within a few minutes a black cab pulled up and the driver asked her where she was going. When she told him, he offered to drive her, but she declined, explaining that she didn't have enough money to cover the fare for the six-mile journey. Claiming to be concerned about a young woman being out by herself late at night, the driver said he would accept the £5 she had on her. Having had a few drinks, she agreed, thinking him plausible and friendly. As a licensed cabbie, he would also have seemed a trustworthy figure to a lone woman aged nineteen on the streets after midnight.

As soon as she was in the car, the driver offered her a cigarette, but he asked her to sit on the floor to smoke it as he did not want to be caught breaking the law, which forbids passengers from smoking in taxis. He then told her he had won a lot of money gambling in a casino and brandished a wad of notes to prove it. Champagne was apparently produced by way of celebration and he invited her to share a glass with him (though it is not clear if the taxi was stopped in order to pour it). Instinctively worried about whether this drink might have been spiked, Carrie tipped it onto the floor as they continued driving along. Then, the conversation took a different turn. The driver told her that he had recently driven a female passenger who had said she would be willing to perform a sex act on him for £350. He asked Carrie if she would consider doing the same thing. She tried to laugh off this suggestion. He persisted, admiring her looks and asking if she had ever done any glamour modelling. He stopped the taxi close to Putney Common, which is within striking distance of East Sheen, allegedly to go to the lavatory. She waited in the cab for him and rang Haiste, telling him what was going on and expressing her doubts about the man's behaviour. She did not leave the cab, however.

After about ten minutes the driver returned, apparently commenting that she 'must be good with alcohol' because she seemed to him to be more sober than he had expected. At this point he is said to have joined her in the back of the cab and dared her to drink a glass of vodka for £10. When she refused, he offered her £50 and a free journey to East Sheen. She acquiesced. Carrie can recall little of what happened after swallowing the drink. She is thought to have staggered through the front door of her mother's house at about 3 a.m. – some ninety minutes after she is understood to have been picked up in Chelsea – vomited and then passed out in a bath. Her mother had no idea what was going on as Carrie was pretty much incoherent. She did not wake up for about twelve hours. Although she believed that she had drunk alcohol which must have been laced with a drug of some kind, she did not report the incident to the police immediately and continued her summer break as planned, including taking up a work experience placement at the PR firm Fishburn Hedges in central London the following month. She did tell friends about her strange taxi journey, of course, but the importance of it would only show itself several months later.

It was not long afterwards that Oliver Haiste and Carrie began dating. Haiste did not attend the University of Warwick, but he was her boyfriend for much of her final two years there, gaining insights into her life as a student. The couple had been introduced in London by their mutual friend – and Carrie's contemporary at Godolphin and Latymer School – Clare Williams during Carrie's first year. 'I met her when she was about nineteen,' Haiste says.

We had friends in common. We had a big mixed group of friends from both sides. It was quite a social relationship. Her friends would date my friends. The first time we met was on the King's Road and we later had a meal in Richmond by the river. Carrie and I got on quite well because we're both vegetarians. We clicked on that. She was always interested in animal rights. She was vegetarian because of her views on animal welfare. She had a Norfolk terrier called Milly-Molly-Mandy, who she called Milly. Her mother wasn't a vegetarian, but she was. We were just friends to begin with and then we went out. I'm older by seven years. I was working in London in public affairs. I would go to Warwick and see her. And she was down in London every other weekend pretty much.

Haiste's recollection is that from her second year onwards, Carrie lived in a flat in Leamington Spa. Her flatmates included Saskia Roddick, who went on to be an actress, and Frances Charles, who had been in the year above Carrie at their prep school, Bute House, and attended St Paul's Girls' School. Miss Charles studied English Literature and went on to work in the international charity sector. 'It was a basic place, just normal student accommodation about ten minutes' walk from the railway station,' says Haiste. 'Carrie was in the lacrosse team at university and they had a very active social life. There was a very lively atmosphere. She seemed to be quite in the heart of the social life there. Alongside Theatre Studies she did one module of History of Art, I think.' He can also recall visiting her at Warwick to watch her perform on stage. 'She was a good actress,' he says. 'I saw her in modern plays. I think I remember some Tom Stoppard being performed.'

Others who also read Theatre Studies are less certain that she did much acting at university, however. One contemporary took the trouble to go back through a list of almost twenty productions staged by the Warwick University Drama Society and two other drama societies, Codpiece and Freshblood. No evidence of Carrie's involvement in any of the plays these amateur companies put on between 2006 and 2009 was found. That is not to say that she was not a member of the society or that she did not play some role in it. The only production in which she is known definitely to have appeared onstage was based on the work of Aleister Crowley, a writer and magician who was born in Leamington Spa in 1875 and who became interested in the occult while at Cambridge. As a young man, Crowley settled in Italy but was expelled from the country after rumours reached the authorities of his drug-taking, orgies and the sacrifice of babies on his property. From then, he sought out notoriety and was referred to in the press as 'the great beast' or 'the wickedest man alive'. He is said to have indulged in sadomasochistic sex rituals with men and women and continued to use hard drugs including cocaine and heroin. It was decided that from this twisted world, enough material could be mined to put on a play. Carrie agreed to be in it and somebody else who was present, perhaps as a member of the audience, took a few photographs. In these amateur shots, she can be seen wearing a black dress and torn black tights. Heavy black make-up is smeared around her eyes. One picture shows her kneeling on the floor with a table in the background. On the table are written the words 'cognac, cunt and cocaine', which feature in Crowley's obscene 666-word poem 'Leah Sublime'. It includes the graphic lines: 'Straddle your Beast, My Masterful Bitch … Spit on me, scarlet, Mouth of my harlot … Soak me in cognac, cunt and cocaine.' A bottle of cognac and small pile of white powder, believed to represent cocaine, can be seen on a table which is surrounded by a circle of cards. The words 'Do As Thou Wilt' are written in chalk in the centre of the circle. Alongside her appears a semi-naked male student with 'The Beast' and 'Do As Thou Wilt' daubed across his chest and throat in black ink. One contemporary who was an acquaintance of Carrie says:

> She didn't act a lot and I don't remember her performing in any plays. I do remember her watching some plays that friends of hers were involved in. I don't remember the Crowley play at all. It could have been part of One World Week, which was an annual drama festival held at Warwick, but it wouldn't have been a studio show, as I would have known about it.

It was in early 2008, midway through Carrie's second year, that a friend, believed to be Clare Williams, who was then studying at Manchester University, contacted her to tell her about a news story of which she had just become aware. On 19 February, a fifty-year-old London taxi driver called John Worboys had appeared in court charged with drugging and sexually assaulting several female passengers in the back of his cab. Details published at the time outlined Worboys's modus operandi: he had offered the women a drink to celebrate an alleged gambling win before launching the attacks. Worboys was remanded in custody and the police made an appeal for other women to contact them if they suspected they had also been assaulted by him. Carrie did not need to be persuaded that she should raise her case from the previous summer. About thirty other women are understood to have come forward at about the same time as her, but Carrie was one of the few able to pick out Worboys from an identification parade. She remembered him as the driver who had taken her from Chelsea to East Sheen in July 2007. When detectives investigated further, they found Worboys had written down Carrie's mobile number and kept it at his house in London. It is not clear how Worboys obtained the number, but this piece of evidence made Carrie, one of his youngest victims, one of the prosecution's star witnesses. Worboys's crown court trial was set for January 2009.

What is perhaps surprising is that while she was a university student, Carrie decided to submit a photograph of herself to *FHM*, the monthly magazine aimed at young men. It was running a competition called High Street Honeys which was described by the organisers as a 'quest to unearth the sexiest "girl next door"'. In the year in which Carrie is believed to have entered this competition, almost 14,000 young women from all over Britain sent photos of themselves in a variety of provocative poses wearing skimpy underwear or a bikini. Their pictures were posted online and members of the public were invited to vote for their favourite. The eventual winner would receive a prize of £10,000 and a twelve-month contract in which she would be trained to become a television presenter. Haiste says:

> I remember it because I told her that on the [FHM] website you could just put your page on a reload to get more votes if you wanted to. There was a way you could do the URL and get it to refresh and then just put the votes up. I remember joking about it at the time, but she said, 'That's quite interesting.' It was an online voting thing. It was one of those fairly naff things. It was her idea to put herself forward. She's always been an attention seeker, there's no denying that. I knew that from Day One.

Carrie was not named Britain's High Street Honey and a lawyer for

Bauer Media, which owned the now-defunct *FHM* magazine, says that all digital material relating to successive High Street Honeys competitions was expunged several years ago. This means that Carrie's blushes have almost certainly been spared, for it seems highly unlikely that the picture in question will ever surface. Furthermore, in June 2021, the *Daily Mail*, which first reported her interest in the High Street Honeys competition, claimed that she had used a European data protection law known as the 'right to be forgotten' to ask search engines like Google to delist certain results for queries relating to her name, suggesting she has given some thought to her past digital activities. Haiste says his memory of the photograph she submitted is hazy and he has trouble describing it. 'She wore something unacceptable,' he says. 'I can't remember what. It certainly wasn't a cardigan and pearls.' He added in a follow-up email: 'The photos that Carrie asked me to send to the so-called lads' mags like *FHM* back in the day were relatively explicit (e.g. bikini and also topless ones).' In 2019, a colleague of Carrie's told *Private Eye*: 'It became an in-joke with friends as she rose up the ranks in Tory HQ, and we'd find the proof on our phones in the pub when people didn't believe us.'

Although the prospect of having to appear at a high-profile trial must have overshadowed much of 2008 and the early part of 2009, Carrie did not let it disrupt her plans. She spent much of the summer of 2008 as an intern at three London PR and communications agencies: Mulberry Marketing Communications, Publicasity and Doner Cardwell Hawkins, confirming that any interest in working in the theatre was drifting further from her mind. It also points to a desire on her part to leave university and join the real world, no doubt spurred on by her relationship with Haiste, who was already well into establishing his own professional career.

John Worboys's trial began early in January 2009 and spanned the next two months. On 13 March 2009, Worboys was found guilty of one rape, five sexual assaults and one attempted assault, as well as twelve charges of drugging lone women passengers. These crimes were found to have been committed between October 2006 and February 2008. Worboys had denied all of these offences. He was cleared of two further drugging charges. During the trial, it was disclosed to Croydon Crown Court that he was a former stripper who had also taken part in a pornographic film. He was revealed to have targeted lone women late at night by offering them a free or discounted lift home, sometimes claiming that he lived nearby. He would then pretend to have won large amounts of money on the lottery or at casinos and ask them to share a glass of champagne with him which had in fact been laced with sedatives, rendering the women defenceless. Many had no idea what had happened to them. Some were left with flashbacks, others with half-memories of Worboys sitting beside them in the back of his taxi.

At the trial, Worboys admitted lying to the women and offering them drinks but maintained he did so because he craved female attention. Despite his defence counsel portraying him as an 'odd-ball' or 'weirdo', it was clear that he was in fact a serial offender who posed a huge threat to women. Police found a so-called rape kit at his house which included gloves, alcohol, glasses, drugs, condoms and a sex toy concealed in a plastic bag. Yet what also emerged from this squalid criminal case was the incompetence of the Metropolitan Police itself. Disturbingly, officers had received reports from various women of assaults or strange experiences in the back of black cabs dating back to 2002 which bore striking similarities, yet nobody had linked them. Worboys had even been arrested in July 2007 after one incident involving a young woman, but he had denied any wrongdoing. The Crown Prosecution Service was not told about this and Worboys was released on bail until, a few months later, the case was dropped. He went on to attack dozens of other women until his arrest in February 2008, which led to the charges on which he was convicted. It is noteworthy that the Mayor of London at the time of Worboys's conviction had the power to demand the sacking of any Metropolitan Police officer who could be shown to have bungled a case. Even in the face of such overwhelming proof of the public having been failed in connection with Worboys, the Mayor did not make any such call. He was, of course, Boris Johnson.

After the trial's conclusion, Carrie, who had been able to give her evidence under the cloak of anonymity, decided to unmask herself. In the days afterwards, interviews with her and details about her appeared on the BBC News website, in the *Daily Mail*, the *Daily Telegraph*, *The Times* and the *Coventry Telegraph*. She discussed her appalling experience openly. For example, in the *Daily Telegraph*, which described her as a 'confident blonde' and listed the name of her school and university, she explained what had happened after Worboys had joined her in the back of his taxi when it was parked near Putney Common and challenged her to drink a shot of vodka.

'I downed it, which was stupid, as I just wanted to get home,' she said. And she told the BBC: 'At every point in the journey I didn't feel like I could demand anything because I felt indebted to him – the fact that he was giving me this journey for £5. He seemed quite friendly. I didn't feel worried by him at any point.' Having explained to the BBC how she had come to drink the vodka, she said:

> I can't remember anything from that point onwards and that's what is so worrying. I believe he got into the front of the cab and did drive me back then straight away. I feel that if I was assaulted I would instinctively know. That's what I hope. But it's awful not to have that peace of mind to know exactly what did happen. I can 99 per cent say nothing happened but to have that 1 per cent of doubt is terrifying.

It is worth pointing out that eighteen months later, on 21 September 2010, the *Evening Standard* published a short clarification which would appear to suggest that the 1 per cent of doubt that had been in her mind may since have been extinguished. The newspaper wrote:

> Last Wednesday we published an article which stated that Caroline Symonds was raped by cab driver John Worboys. We would like to make clear that this was incorrect and that Caroline (pictured) was not raped. In fact she escaped from Worboys after he spiked her drink and showed courage in coming forward to help to bring him to justice. We apologise for the distress caused by our error.

When the proceedings ended in March 2009, she also spoke of the burden she had felt at having to appear at the trial. Many women had told the police they felt sure they had been attacked by Worboys but they had no evidence to support their claims, preventing their cases from full consideration in court. She said she felt angry that Worboys had not pleaded guilty, forcing her and other victims to testify. 'I was nervous about giving evidence,' she said. 'I feel I was representing a lot of girls who were not going to stand in court. I felt happy with how it went in court. I broke down afterwards.' She said of Worboys: 'He is a very sad, deluded person and he is a danger to society. I hate that it's been played down that he is just a weirdo. He is more than a weirdo, he is very, very dangerous.' She told the BBC that she was considering a career in the media or marketing but admitted that she was dogged by the question of what had happened to her. 'It's terrible to think I will never ever know and there's nothing I can do about it,' she said. 'To hear other stories of girls who can't remember what happened and thought nothing happened and then to find buttons missing off their skirt and such like that – it's a terrifying thought and obviously you think all of the worst things.'

On 21 April, Worboys was jailed indefinitely and told he must serve a minimum of eight years. The judge at Croydon Crown Court, Mr Justice Penry-Davey, said he would not be released until a parole board decided he no longer presented a threat to women. No doubt delighted that the trial was behind her, and pleased to be able to focus on enjoying her final term at university, Carrie belatedly celebrated her 21st birthday the following week in a restaurant in Leamington Spa with her mother and a small group of friends. Her flatmate, Frances Charles, gave a short speech in which she praised Carrie. 'You're just that little bit more fabulous than every-body else,' Miss Charles said, evidently speaking from the heart. 'Things are never mundane with you. They are exciting, they can be very frustrating, but they are never ever dull.' By way of illustration, she told a vignette of how Carrie's idea of supermarket shopping for household 'essentials' had recently involved her buying noth-ing more than '300 ice lollies and six bottles of £80 champagne'. If nothing else, Miss Charles mentioning this showed that even as a university student, Carrie's attitude to money was considerably more relaxed than her flatmate's.

Two further amusing anecdotes followed. 'Carrie had her first kiss aged sixteen and has been steadily making up for it ever since,' said Miss Charles. 'In fact, when Carrie was looking at the guest list for the party, she remarked to her mother: "I've pulled most of the people coming. Sixteen in fact."' Miss Charles went on: 'After about two hours of a sort of strained silence and offish behaviour from Carrie's mother, Carrie realised that she hadn't explained herself properly and that to pull someone meant just kiss. And it had to be made clear that Carrie hadn't in fact slept with over fifteen people.' Continuing with this theme, Miss Charles also told how Carrie had recently attended a friend's party and flirted with the host's young cousin. 'Clearly Carrie's memories of being a late developer in the kissing world have come back to haunt her,' said Miss Charles.

She met a young man – good looking, well dressed, cousin of the host of the party – who to her surprise told her: 'I've never been kissed before.' And Carrie, in a fit of powerful generosity, said: 'Well, how would you like your first kiss to be with a beautiful twenty-year-old?' He obviously accepted and a wonderful time was had by Carrie... and said thirteen-year-old!

Showing genuine concern for her friend, Miss Charles did turn briefly to the Worboys case, rounding off her speech by saying: 'You have been incredibly brave over the last few months with everything that's been going on and you've handled yourself with enviable poise and dignity throughout and I'm so proud of you.' In response, Carrie stood and spoke for a few seconds. 'I'm a bit pissed,' she admitted.

The first thing that's really important [to say] is, don't we all look really bloody good tonight? I actually meant that, because a couple of my home friends have come up to me and said, 'You said that Warwick was a really monstrous university,' which it is, let's be honest ... And I'd like to say my friends are only very, very, very fit, so well done for being here. Cheers!

Carrie took a First Class degree in Theatre Studies and History of Art in June 2009. She has remained close to some of those who attended Warwick at the same time as her and is known to have made a return visit to her alma mater at least once since leaving. Showing the kind of ambition for which she has become well known, though, she did not rest on her laurels when she had completed her studies. In July 2009, just a few weeks after graduating, she secured her first job in London, working as an account executive at Mulberry Marketing Communications. Her move towards creating and controlling messages had begun.

CHAPTER 4

INTO POLITICS

The tremors caused by the financial crash of 2007 and 2008 were still being felt in the summer of 2009. Indeed, it would be 2013 before the British economy returned to its pre-recession size, meaning that jobs were less plentiful than they had been, particularly for inexperienced graduates. Carrie did not seem to let this turbulence worry her, however. Within a few months of arriving at Mulberry Marketing Communications she had defied these unfavourable conditions to secure employment at Lansons, a rival public relations firm based in Clerkenwell, where she was one of a handful of graduate trainees to be hired in November 2009. Tony Langham, the company's co-founder, says she began working in public relations and then moved into public affairs as a junior executive learning the ropes. 'She's one of the graduate trainees that I remember,' says Langham. 'She's got a huge personality. She was good at her job. She stood out.'

While helping to oversee business accounts might have been considered heavy going for any 21-year-old whose chief concern until only a few months before had been Theatre Studies, this would have been an excellent training ground on which to sharpen her prospects in an industry that can reward its best practitioners handsomely. It is surprising to discover, therefore, that she stuck at this job for less than a year. By September 2010, she had left. It is not as if she traded in the security of a steady salary for nothing, but it is fair to say that her next career move – into politics – came as a mild shock to some of those who were closest to her at the time.

The period in which she worked for Lansons was one in which politics was at the forefront of the national consciousness thanks to the 2010 general election. Gordon Brown, the sitting Labour Prime Minister, had come to be seen as a man whose powers were waning after more than a decade in government. For the first time since 1992, it was widely felt that the Conservatives, now under the comparatively youthful David Cameron, had a realistic prospect of forming the next government. With each of the main parties having changed their leader since the previous election in 2005, an unusually large number of MPs choosing not to seek re-election, and televised debates between the main parties taking place for the first time, the May 2010 poll was certainly not short of intrigue. That it resulted in a hung parliament made it even more fascinating. The country was briefly gripped by uncertainty until, after five days of tense negotiations, it was announced that there would be a coalition government headed by Cameron and supported by Nick Clegg, the leader of the Liberal Democrats, as his Deputy Prime Minister. It is not clear to what degree any of this excitement featured on Carrie's radar. According to electoral roll records held by the London Borough of Richmond upon Thames, the local authority covering East

Sheen, where she lived, the only person who was registered to vote at her home address was her mother.

Yet in the run-up to the poll, and in its immediate aftermath, Carrie was offered several opportunities by Oliver Haiste, her semi-regular boyfriend between 2007 and 2012, to peer into the world of Westminster. Haiste, an instinctive Conservative with Eurosceptic leanings, describes himself as having been something of a good-humoured 'political ranter' during their relationship. Through his own work in public affairs and with several years' head-start on Carrie in full-time employment, he had made some useful political contacts. 'Carrie wasn't naturally politically inclined,' he says of that period. 'She didn't have passionate political views. She wasn't ideologically driven. At university she wasn't a member of a debating society or into politics or journalism at all. She certainly wasn't a William Hague-type figure,' he adds, in reference to the former Tory leader who famously addressed the 1977 Conservative Party conference when he was sixteen years old. Neither, he thinks, was her mother noticeably politically active, meaning that politics did not play an especially important role in her household.

If Carrie was less interested in politics than Haiste, however, she did not let it show. 'In those early days I introduced her to members of Conservative Future, the youth wing of the party, and she got to know some people,' he remembers. 'I even took her to a few meetings with Lord Pearson of Rannoch, who was, briefly, the leader of UKIP.' By far the most useful connection Haiste was able to make for Carrie came at a party held in Richmond shortly after the election. It was hosted by Haiste's friend Zeno Goldsmith, who is a couple of years older than Carrie and a member of one of Britain's most prominent and influential families, which seems effortlessly to straddle business, politics and society. Zeno's father was the late Teddy Goldsmith, the environmentalist and a founding editor of *The Ecologist* magazine; his uncle was the late financier Sir James Goldsmith; and his first cousin is the politician Zac (now Lord) Goldsmith. At the point when Zeno threw his party, Zac had recently been elected as the new Conservative MP for the key marginal constituency of Richmond Park, making him Carrie's MP. Haiste, Carrie and Zeno apparently began talking about politics. 'Zeno mentioned that Zac was potentially looking for assistants,' remembers Haiste. Carrie did not waste any time, it seems. The same month that she left Lansons she began working for Goldsmith as his campaign and marketing director. Tony Langham, her boss at Lansons, says that, looking back, her departure from the firm makes sense to him in professional terms. 'She was clearly destined for big things and she clearly wanted to get there quickly, so I probably wasn't so surprised that she left,' he comments. 'It sounded a more senior job. She had the word "director" in the title. She just had that air about her of wanting to make progress as quickly as possible.' To this day, Carrie's loyalty to the man who gave her this crucial break burns brightly, and she credits him with her decision to work for the Conservative Party.

In the autumn of 2010, Zac Goldsmith cut a distinctive and rather glamorous figure in British politics generally and in the Conservative Party in particular. Thirty-five years old, highly articulate, independently wealthy and well connected, he was described in some quarters as the Conservatives' 'green conscience' because of his passion for defending animal rights and protecting the environment. The contest that saw him wrestle back Richmond Park for the Tories for the first time since 1997 had been a bad-tempered affair. In the course of it, Susan Kramer, who had held the seat for the Liberal Democrats since 2005, had accused him of trying to 'buy' his way to Westminster by using his own money to fund his campaign. Goldsmith had labelled her an 'attack dog' who told 'the most appalling lies'. He also claimed the Liberal Democrats had tried to 'kneecap' him by tearing down his election posters and, allegedly, trying to infiltrate his campaign team. Hostilities rarely let up, and even though Goldsmith had emerged the clear winner with a majority of 4,091 and a swing in his direction of 7 per cent, he remained alert to the fact that victory next time was by no means assured. For this reason, he was happy to have energetic people around him to help boost his profile and entrench his position. Carrie fitted the bill perfectly.

Despite her lack of political experience, it is easy to see why her head was turned by Goldsmith in a professional sense, allowing her to alter the direction of her career. Not only do she and Goldsmith share to this day an interest in 'green' issues, but the Conservatives' Richmond Park constituency office is located in the Upper Richmond Road, just a short stroll from where she was living with her mother. According to Oliver Haiste, Goldsmith's chosen political affiliation was almost incidental to Carrie, who, he believes, was not driven in those days in any obvious way by a clear set of political beliefs. 'I think the fact Zac was round the corner made her think, "I might as well,"' says Haiste.

She is essentially apolitical. She was a fairly blank canvas. It's all about the Conservative Party, but for what reason? It's like supporting a football club. There's no reason for it. It just becomes a colour you attach yourself to. That's how it was with Carrie. Many political activists are like that now.

She was not the only young woman who had begun working for Goldsmith, who also ran a private office overlooking Richmond Green. At this time, she met and became friendly with another member of his local support team, Theodora Clarke, who has been the MP for Stafford since 2019.

Within a few weeks of starting her duties for Goldsmith, Carrie was invited to attend the Conservative Party's annual conference in Birmingham. There, she made what was almost certainly her first – albeit unofficial – statement on behalf of the organisation that has come to define so much of her professional life. It came during a short exchange with Brian Reade, a reporter from her grandfather's old newspaper, the left-leaning *Daily Mirror*, who was writing a tongue-in-cheek sketch about young Conservatives. 'I speak to a couple of them – Theodora Clarke and Carrie Symonds, hard-working, on-the-ball gals with accents as far back as the Dark Ages,' Reade wrote.

Whatever happened to those young Tories who gave us such fun with their drunken frolics, I ask. 'We're not a social club any more,' says Theodora, who works for Zac Goldsmith. 'It's much more serious now. There's a feeling that if we behave seriously we'll be taken seriously.' 'Yah,' says Carrie. 'We're serious now.

There's a different feel. We don't hold meetings in bars. We have coffee mornings.'

It remains unclear how many Conservative coffee mornings Carrie had attended by this point and equally hard to establish whether she was paid out of public funds for the few months in which she was engaged by Goldsmith to oversee his marketing push in Richmond. During that time, his local concerns included a campaign to stop three blocks of flats being built near Twickenham station; a lengthy negotiation with Thames Water over the construction of a new sewer; and a campaign to make the London 2012 Olympics plastic bag-free. It seems likely that Carrie might have had some involvement in using these somewhat humdrum matters to boost Goldsmith's profile locally. Oliver Haiste is under the impression that she may have had a temporary contract of some description while assisting him in his duties. Having left the security of Lansons of her own volition, it would seem unlikely that she worked for Goldsmith primarily for the financial reward, though. Rather, it appears that she had an eye on the future, having realised that politics might be her calling. 'Her relationship with politics, at that time at least, was career-driven rather than ideological,' Haiste says. This assertion would appear to ring true on the basis of what happened next.

Sometime around Christmas 2010, Carrie got wind of the fact that Conservative Party campaign headquarters (CCHQ) was seeking to hire a new press officer at its operation in Millbank Tower, close to the Houses of Parliament. The post paid a salary of about

£25,000. Henry Macrory was in charge of the press office and over-saw the recruitment process. 'Carrie applied for a job as a press officer at Conservative campaign headquarters in early 2011,' he recalls.

A vacancy had arisen and I asked her to come in for an interview. I had intended to give the job to another excellent candidate, but Carrie's CV stood out. She'd had political experience working for Zac Goldsmith in Richmond, and she had a talent for writing. I interviewed her at CCHQ with my deputy, Zoe Thorogood. We both thought she was an outstanding candidate. She was clever, charming and confident, and fizzed with vitality. I remember her telling us how much she liked writing. She was an extremely impressive interviewee. I'd earmarked someone else for the po-sition, but I said to Zoe after the interview that I didn't think we could afford to let Carrie slip through the net. She agreed, and I rang Carrie the next day to tell her she'd got the job.

On the cusp of celebrating her 23rd birthday, Carrie's small career gamble had paid off. There is no question that by manoeuvring herself into a position where she was able to work for Goldsmith for a short period of time, she killed two birds with one stone, successfully adding a political dimension to her portfolio while guaranteeing she would hear of other opportunities higher up the tree in the same organisation. She had climbed a couple of rungs of the ladder in the space of six months. Another source who worked in the Conservative Party's press office in 2011 says that Carrie's achievement in being offered a post there at the first attempt was all the more impressive because the candidate whom she leapfrogged in order to secure it was Camilla Groom, who was arguably better qualified. Groom's CV is said to have included a spell working for Barack Obama. As it transpired, Groom was offered another job in the Tory press office not long after Carrie was hired, and she and Carrie went on to become friends. In 2018, Groom married Will Walden, a former BBC producer who served as a senior adviser to Boris Johnson between 2012 and 2019. 'I remember that Carrie and Camilla used to sit next to each other at CCHQ,' says the source. 'They got on well and Camilla also later worked for Boris.'

When political parties are in government, the importance of their own press operation quite naturally diminishes. This means that the work of a party press officer can be quite restricted and rather less fun than when a well-run party is engaged in a keenly fought battle to return to power. 'When you're in government, the press office is tiny,' says one former Conservative press officer. 'It's only about six people strong. It's not the same as when you're in opposition. When I worked there in the approach to the 2010 general election campaign, and in the three or four years before then, there were about twenty-five of us.' Another former staffer says: 'The party press office takes on more of a supporting role when you're in government, focusing on local elections, by-elections and general party business. There's no question it is less exciting and probably less social because there are fewer people around.'

Still, Carrie seized with both hands the opportunity she had carved out for herself, and some remember her being conspicuous for her attentiveness. One seasoned political figure recalls encountering her in those early days and thinking her unusually competent and proactive for a Tory press officer at that time. A fourth person who worked in CCHQ when she arrived says: 'She was very green when she turned up. She knew little about the media but was keen to be involved.'

Her move into a new political job in 2011 came shortly before other changes in her life. At her suggestion, she and Haiste split up after more than three years together. Although he says the romance was rekindled briefly in 2012, this initial break was ultimately conclusive. 'The relationship was tumultuous,' Haiste admits.

We always knew there was a natural compatibility, but the relationship just wasn't functioning. We were just arguing too much. It was quite standard for her to lose her temper. Massively so. She lost her temper plenty of times with me. Sometimes I had to leave the house. There were slamming doors.

Haiste says that it would not be proper for him to expand further, but he will admit that the problems they went through ranged from being rather trivial to, on occasion, having more serious consequences. 'I remember when we went to Kenya she cried because her hair straighteners didn't work. We were on safari and going to the beach for two weeks. And she had a big strop in Paris once because I wasn't enjoying myself. I don't much like the place.' He goes on to confirm that her anger occasionally spilled over into outright volatility and he acknowledges that it would be fair to describe Carrie as a 'live wire'. In his opinion, her friends and her mother would recognise this description as well. 'I remember in her house having arguments. I'd say: 'Be quiet, your mum's upstairs,' and she wouldn't care. Usually when you have a row and someone else is there you keep it quiet. But she didn't really mind too much.' He says the arguments could take place 'on the turn of a coin or [as a result of] some minor thing which then brought up fundamental issues'.

Despite these intermittent rough patches, he speaks fondly of his former girlfriend and says that when things were on an even keel, the relationship worked well. They would travel widely and had a mutual love of films, especially psychological thrillers.

There was a lot of passion, a lot of affection, a lot of shared tastes. She was very fun, engaging, affectionate, exciting. She always wanted to do things, always wanted to go places. It was never a lazy relationship. Messages [from her] weren't generic. They were very specific. Things like: 'I saw this which reminded me of you...' That type of thing. She was thoughtful. We went on holidays to Kenya, to Egypt, to Italy quite a few times and also made several trips to Prague. And we'd travel within Britain. We reignited the relationship in 2012 but it just petered out. We never talked about marriage. Well, only in a hypothetical sense. She did once tell me what her three children were going to be called. Wilfred wasn't among the names. She said she wanted three children: Poppy for a girl and Monty for a boy. I can't remember the third name.

Signs of her temper being less than serene at all times manifested in mood swings. One source says: 'She could be quite complicated.

Everyone knew that.' Haiste says that he was not the only person with whom she had tiffs. 'She and [her school friend] Clare Williams had a big falling out,' he remarks.

> It must have been a couple of years after she'd left university. They just stopped talking. I'm not sure of the specifics. What you'll find with Carrie is a lot of burnt bridges along the way. You'll notice a lot of intense friendships that peter out very quickly. That's the pattern, in my view. The same happened with a girl she lived with at Warwick. Difficult people quite often bring with them quite a lot of charisma, which is why they're enticing and exciting to be with. Undoubtedly she was a difficult person. I don't think anyone would deny that. She'd probably admit that herself.

This account is bolstered by a second source who says that Carrie and Frances Charles, who, as mentioned in the previous chapter, shared a flat with her at university and gave a speech at Carrie's 21st birthday party, had a significant falling out. The source would not be drawn on why this might have happened.

Haiste adds that he believes Carrie was motivated by a desire to be famous. 'She's got plenty of charisma. She was able to be tough if required. She could very easily push herself to extremes if she needed to. I think she needs validation, hence the attention-seeking.' He says that this perceived hunger to be noticed overrode any serious interest in money on her part. Nor, he says, did she show any sign of being a snob. 'She was never interested in grand houses and titles. She never asked people what school they went to or anything.'

Sometime after she and Haiste went their separate ways, Carrie became close to Tim Dixon, an exact contemporary of hers from the University of Warwick. He worked for a marketing agency in London, but the relationship is not thought to have been particularly serious. Seemingly, her priorities lay elsewhere, specifically in finding her feet and in getting to know her new colleagues. As one former CCHQ staffer notes:

> Unlike others, she hadn't worked with us during the recent general election campaign, so she was considered to be a bit of an outsider. And she'd taken this slightly unusual route into CCHQ, because most of us had worked in the media or for an MP in the House of Commons. She had done neither. She was keen to get ahead, I remember that. She was driven. She wanted to be noticed despite her lack of experience.

Another says that the hierarchy that existed tended to be based around the length of time served. 'To fit in, you had to be helpful and do your best without putting noses out of joint by outshining those who'd been there longer than you. It was quite small "p" political in that sense.'

The Conservatives' office in the Millbank Tower complex certainly lacked the grandeur of one of the party's earlier bases, in nearby Smith Square, though it had at least been refurbished after the lease had been signed in 2006. Nor was it brilliantly located, being a ten-minute walk from the Houses of Parliament and further still from the centre of power in Downing Street. The closest government departments to the complex are the Department for

Transport and the Home Office. It was, says one who worked there for several years, slightly out on a limb in relation to the rest of Westminster. Lunching options in the complex were limited, too, consisting of a branch of Pizza Express and a sandwich bar. This meant that socially minded young staffers were always happy to walk to the nearest pubs, such as the Marquis of Granby or The Speaker.

Having begun to get to grips with the requirements of her job and been accepted into the Conservative Party fold, in late 2011 she was seconded onto Boris Johnson's campaign to be re-elected as the Mayor of London. After four years in post, Johnson was thought to have a fair chance of retaining the job and therefore of serving a second successive term, meaning that plenty of resources went into the effort to keep him in place. Polls showed him to be more popular in London than the Conservative Party, while his main opponent, Ken Livingstone, was less popular than the Labour Party. Carrie was part of a little unit within CCHQ that was overseen by Lynton Crosby, the Australian political strategist, providing her with her first taste of working under the rigours of an election drive.

If she ever did catch her future husband's eye at this early stage of her career, she is not thought to have held his attention for long. As his campaign burst into life, he was becoming closer to another woman in her twenties, Jennifer Arcuri, despite still being married to his second wife, Marina Wheeler. Arcuri, an American student, had moved to London in 2011 in an attempt to start a technology business and had first met Johnson on 13 October that year at a British Venture Capital Association reception held at the

Landmark Hotel in Marylebone. In March 2012, two months before polling day, she managed to secure a seat on Johnson's election campaign bus as a volunteer and sat within his eyeline, capturing his attention. Some of his aides noticed the flirtation, but they were probably unaware that at the end of the journey she gave Johnson her telephone number. He rang her shortly afterwards. She was even photographed posing provocatively alongside him during the campaign wearing a blue T-shirt bearing the slogan 'Back Boris'. In the early hours of 4 May, it was announced that Johnson had won the election by 62,538 votes. He would remain the Mayor of London until 2016 and over the course of his second term would also become a frequent visitor to Miss Arcuri's rented top-floor flat in Shoreditch High Street in east London. All of this was far outside of Carrie's orbit. Her focus at the time was on shoring up her position as a junior political aide.

By the time she had worked at CCHQ for almost eighteen months, it would have been evident to Carrie that there were three branches to the professional tree that had to be climbed. Building the relationships that would allow her to do so took time. Firstly, as a press officer, it was essential for her to mix with journalists, principally those who worked in the Lobby. She needed to get to know them primarily so that she could place stories in the newspapers for which they wrote. The fact that the journalists would also tell her anecdotes about what was going on in and around Westminster was a very useful by-product of this arrangement and it cut both ways: many in the Lobby realised that it would be in their interests to know her because, whether she knew it or not, she could also furnish them with ideas and material which are the lifeblood of their trade.

For this arrangement to work as well as possible from her point of view, it was also important for her to know as many special advisers – the political appointees hired to support government ministers – as possible. Special advisers, known as spads, represented the second branch of the tree. By rubbing shoulders with them, she would come to hear even more gossip about what was happening in politics as well as potentially placing herself in contention to become a spad at some point in the future.

The third branch of the tree could be said to be represented by the politicians themselves, together with their closest staff. Some colleagues remember that she made little attempt to disguise her ambition when it came to getting to know them. Having settled in easily to the Westminster scene, she soon marked herself out as an assiduous networker, socialising regularly with colleagues, reporters, special advisers and even senior politicians who might usually be considered above the station of a relatively junior press officer. One figure who worked with her in CCHQ for several years echoes this. 'It was a funny time because [CCHQ] was all a bit fractious and rudderless from about 2013 onwards,' he says.

She was very bright, pretty and engaging and a lot of fun to work with. I don't think she particularly enjoyed the duller side of the job, like getting press releases out, but she was by far the best person to get you good gossip on what was going on and liked to spend time with journalists.

In early February 2013, the former Liberal Democrat Cabinet minister Chris Huhne resigned his seat in the House of Commons following a scandal in which, a decade earlier, he had pretended that his wife, Vicky Pryce, had been driving a speeding car when in fact he had been at the wheel. This deception was carried out by the couple to spare Huhne, who had accumulated points for speeding already, from being banned from driving for six months. When the truth belatedly came to light, Huhne was charged with perverting the course of justice and was forced to quit as an MP, triggering a by-election in the constituency of Eastleigh in Hampshire. '[Carrie] was doing press stuff down there,' remembers one colleague.

> I'm pretty sure Beth Armstrong and Jacob Willmer were there too. Everyone found it a miserable experience. I'm sure she did as well. By-elections aren't much fun. The Conservative candidate, Maria Hutchings, was a tricky character. She needed to be quite carefully handled. At the count she needed to be shepherded out of the camp and I'm sure Carrie was one of the people soldiering her through the crowd.

Although the Tories had hoped to snatch the seat from the Liberal Democrats, they failed to do so, trailing in third behind the incumbent party, which retained the seat, and UKIP, which was by then eating into the Tory vote as often as not across the country. Eastleigh was the closest three-way result in an English by-election for almost a century. Despite her party's loss, though, Carrie's involvement in the campaign almost certainly improved her prospects within CCHQ, which was by then being run jointly by co-chairmen Lord Feldman and Grant Shapps.

Not long afterwards, while still in her mid-twenties, she was promoted to become the Conservatives' head of broadcast, giving her responsibility for liaising with media organisations which wanted to book Tory MPs to appear as interviewees on their television and radio programmes. On the face of it, this was certainly a vote of confidence in a young CCHQ employee who was less experienced than some of her peers, even if it is widely acknowledged that the job itself is perhaps not quite as senior as outsiders might believe. 'If a party is in power, as the Conservatives were then, party headquarters becomes a bit of a backwater,' says a former colleague who worked in Downing Street at the time.

Most of the communications stuff would go through No. 10, so there wasn't a huge amount of focus for the media at CCHQ at that time. It wasn't a bad training ground, but it's not a place where you'd put your most senior person. It's where you'd put someone who was bright enough to learn the ropes.

Another former colleague says:

Basically, she was dealing with the tier below the Cabinet. There was a head of broadcast in No. 10, who was Michael Salter. She did the CCHQ stuff, so she wouldn't have had to worry about getting people onto *The Andrew Marr Show*, but she would go through the list just below Cabinet level, working out who should go on what shows and taking bids from broadcasters. It meant having a decent enough relationship with broadcasters for *Any Questions* or *The World at One* on Radio 4, telling them, 'This is the best minister we can find for you today', and so on. It was up to her to locate a minister who was well briefed rather than just ringing round any old minister or MP who was happy to go on TV and chat.

As she grew in confidence, she began to earn a reputation among some of her workmates as someone who could be accused of allowing her aspirations to get the better of her. Whether this signified envy or genuine disapproval on their part – or a combination of both – is hard to glean. 'She was very good at playing the Westminster game of having great relationships with a few very senior journalists and good relationships with politicians who then became very popular', reflects one former press officer who worked closely with her for several years.

She has authentic friends like Zac Goldsmith and Josh Grimstone, who eventually became her deputy head of broadcast and who now works for Michael Gove, but she definitely appeared more transactional in some of her Westminster relationships, even by Westminster standards. That was obvious. I also think people who worked with her would acknowledge that she rested very heavily on them to do things.

Another former colleague is at pains to project a more positive memory of her. 'We'd go for drinks after work because we were a group of people in their twenties with time on their hands after working long days,' they say.

> It was quite social. She always had people she got on with and others she didn't, but she was always very good company and good fun, which matters in politics because, as you know, there are more bad days than good. I've always liked her, but I'm not sure if people who've had to manage her and work with her have.

By the time of her promotion, she was in a relationship with her colleague Jacob Willmer, who had worked in the Conservative Party press office since 2008. In May 2013, Willmer went to work as a communications adviser in Somalia and did not return to London until the following year. Carrie spent most of August 2013 on a summer holiday in Sri Lanka with some friends. Subsequently, she struck up a close friendship with another colleague, Elliott Burton, who joined CCHQ as a press officer around the time Willmer left. Her relationship with Burton is understood to have lasted for a shorter period than that with Willmer.

As the 2013 Conservative Party conference appeared on the horizon, Carrie was involved in an amusing instance of low-level skulduggery that has remained lodged in the mind of one CCHQ colleague for its creativity as much as for being a potential indicator of her not wanting to get her hands too dirty in a job that is not famed for its glamour. 'There was a bit of an argument about which hotel CCHQ people would stay in,' this person remembers.

We'd been shoved in a crap hotel on the other side of town from the main conference venue. A few days before conference began, Carrie walked into work with a crutch claiming she'd suffered a fracture to her leg which didn't require a bandage or cast but did mean she couldn't walk without a crutch and consequently couldn't stay far away from the venue. Inevitably she was bumped up to the nice hotel near the conference centre. When conference came, the injury magically healed and she didn't need to use the crutch. I think there was a lot of smiling and an acknowledgment that that's Carrie. She was fun, funny and enthusiastic and is certainly a character. But I would say she was as disliked as much as she was liked, it was 50/50.

It had been announced in 2012 that Lynton Crosby had been hired to run the Conservative Party's next general election campaign, which, under the Fixed Term Parliaments Act, would not take place until May 2015. Crosby took up his post on a part-time basis in 2013 and then worked full-time throughout 2014 right up until polling day. One lesson that had been learned from the 2010 campaign was that, mistakenly, there had been no single campaign manager in charge. Steve Hilton, George Osborne, Andy Coulson and, to some degree, Stephen Gilbert were of similar status and had disagreed on various key matters which had made the 2010 strategy hazy and contributed to the inconclusive result. For that reason, it was understood that in 2015, Crosby was in charge. Appointing him early on and giving him meaningful authority was a very deliberate decision. Yet it was not without consequence for thrusting young

CCHQ employees like Carrie, who, some colleagues sensed, grew ever more eager to move up the chain of command and closer to power. A former CCHQ source says:

> Once Lynton took over, there was an edict that government ministers could no longer hire people from CCHQ as spads. So there were people who'd probably done a couple of years and would want to move who suddenly found they could not. If at any time Carrie seemed frustrated, that might have been the reason. The CCHQ press office could probably do that to you.

Carrie, an inveterate traveller, found other ways to keep herself amused as her time in CCHQ wore on. In the space of the first six months of 2014, she went on trips with friends and colleagues to Dublin, Morocco, the Cotswolds, Spain, Vienna and Moldova. One of these trips may have been work-related. In between came another by-election campaign, in Newark. It was caused by the resignation of the Conservative MP Patrick Mercer, who had been compromised by a lobbying scandal. Significant resources were ploughed into getting his eventual successor, Robert Jenrick, elected. Carrie was part of the team from CCHQ which was sent north to ensure Jenrick's safe passage into Parliament and was photographed on the stump with Priti Patel. Both Patel and Jenrick would go on to be important allies to Carrie in the years to come. Yet some had detected a mild weariness in her enthusiasm for political campaigning by this point. Her forte, they sensed, was in working her contacts in London, where it had not gone unnoticed that she enjoyed eating in fashionable restaurants like the Chiltern

Firehouse in Marylebone. Senior figures recall that she was good at placing stories with journalists – often using her flirtatious manner to good effect – but was not considered a strategic thinker.

Summer in Westminster tends to be a quieter time, and Carrie was able to take holidays in Dorset and Croatia before embarking on a mini-break to Rome in September. This was followed in October by weekends away in Sussex, Norfolk and Vienna. That month she was also a guest at the Institute of Directors in Pall Mall for the 10th anniversary banquet of the political website Guido Fawkes, with whose staff she had by then developed more than a passing acquaintance. Having been established in 2004 by Paul Staines, Guido Fawkes's influence had become significant, even if some of its journalistic methods were considered by certain Fleet Street journalists to be unorthodox. Contrary to what some may perceive, the website did not discriminate when it came to selecting its targets. Indeed, it seemed to specialise in so-called 'blue-on-blue' attacks – that is to say, stories about Conservative Party infighting. It was happy to run scandal stories that compromised the Tories as well as their opponents.

Only a few weeks before the anniversary banquet, for example, the Conservative Minister for Civil Society, Brooks Newmark, had resigned after a Guido Fawkes sting operation which relied heavily on subterfuge and whose ethics are still debated today. In what was billed as an 'investigation', Alex Wickham, a 23-year-old Guido Fawkes reporter, had posed as a Conservative Party activist, setting up a fake Twitter account under the false name Sophie Wittams, who was described as a 'twentysomething Tory PR girl'. Several Tory MPs were contacted by 'Sophie' without any of them responding in anything but a perfunctory way. Newmark, a married father of five, did exchange publicly visible messages with 'Sophie' before entering into a private conversation on WhatsApp which turned increasingly explicit. 'Sophie' sent a picture of a naked woman to Newmark, who, believing the picture to be genuine, promised not to show it to anyone else and said he would send something in return. Subsequently, he sent a graphic photo of himself back. Wickham had his scoop. Two newspapers, including the *Mail on Sunday*, declined to publish any of this on the exclusive basis on which they were offered it by Guido Fawkes. But another paper, the *Sunday Mirror*, opted to run the story on the eve of that year's Conservative Party conference, prompting Newmark's immediate resignation.

In an article for the *Daily Telegraph* published just after the Guido Fawkes 10th anniversary party, the political journalist Peter Oborne noted that Boris Johnson, various Cabinet ministers, some Labour grandees and a group of famous broadcasters had all been in attendance, also revealing that the then Prime Minister David Cameron had even sent a pre-recorded speech which was played to those present. Oborne, too, had been invited to the gathering, but it seemed he used the occasion for his own journalistic purposes. He poured scorn on Guido Fawkes rather than cheering the achievements of Paul Staines, its founder. 'They assembled to celebrate a man whose controversial journalistic techniques destroyed the career of Tory minister Brooks Newmark, who was sent obscene photographs of a woman's private parts over the internet in order to encourage him to do the same,' Oborne raged. 'The story was so far beyond the pale that two national newspapers refused to publish it.' Oborne went on:

Rogue politician Boris Johnson declared that Guido Fawkes was the 'dung that sustains the rosebush of democracy'. He also told the audience something they all privately knew: they had accepted Guido's invitation partly in the hope it might encourage him not to rifle through their dustbins, yet knowing it would probably make not a jot of difference. It is the kind of fearlessness and ruthless for which Fawkes might be admired by some. There is, however, a danger for any journalist in bringing together all his or her friends and contacts under one roof. It tells them more about you than you wish them, and the world, to know.

That Carrie was among the throng certainly showed she was by this point considered – at least by Paul Staines and his young colleague Alex Wickham – to be a player among what could be called the Westminster elite. By December 2014, she had begun a new relationship with another member of the small Guido Fawkes team, Harry Cole, who was then its news editor. That month, she and Cole went to Paris together for a short break and spent the Christmas holidays in Dorset. Cole's own commitment to networking meant he was also making a name for himself in Westminster. Indeed, despite being only two years Carrie's senior, Cole had already managed to secure a place in *Who's Who*, arguably Britain's most revered book of biographical reference, where he described his recreations in one word: 'gossip'. (He later updated his entry to list 'countryside, Pomerol and politics'.) He is thought to have been accorded this honour thanks to his position at Guido Fawkes.

While Carrie was busy forging strong links in media circles, though, not every one of her colleagues at CCHQ felt that she had earned her place at the top table quite yet. 'She was optimistic, a pretty girl and perhaps there weren't many others who were as engaging as her,' reflects one who worked with her at the time. 'But I suppose she was what you might call "big on campus" – in other words, she was successful in a small environment.' Another former CCHQ staffer says:

> I remember once, she'd been out at a meeting and bounced back into the office saying, 'I think I've met someone who has my dream job.' I asked what her dream job was and she said, 'I've met the political editor of *Tatler*.' That's always been very much her. She likes politics but enjoys the social side of things too.

Whatever the reservations of some of her workmates, though, Carrie was determined to make her mark on the political scene and knew that she was unlikely to achieve that aim as a mere press officer. For her, the only way was up.

CHAPTER 5

SPAD

The Conservatives' victory in the 2015 general election took most people around the country and, indeed, in Westminster by surprise. A second successive hung parliament had been widely anticipated after five years of coalition government. In the event, the electorate rejected decisively the offerings both of the Liberal Democrats, whose popularity collapsed, and of the Labour Party, whose leader, Ed Miliband, was widely ridiculed during the campaign for unveiling a nine-foot stone tablet with six election promises carved into it. David Cameron emerged as the party leader with the largest share of the vote, giving him a working majority of twelve seats. For some politicians, the surprises continued. Within a couple of days of victory being declared, John Whittingdale, an MP since 1992 who had not been tipped for Cabinet promotion, received a telephone call from Cameron's chief of staff, Ed Llewellyn, that was to have implications for Carrie.

'Rather to my amazement, Ed Llewellyn rang me saying the Prime Minister was going to appoint me as Secretary of State for Culture, Media and Sport,' recollects Whittingdale.

I moved into the department and one of the first things I was told was that I could have two special advisers [spads]. I didn't have any particular people in mind, but I then received strong recommendations that Carrie would be extremely good. One recommendation was from David Cameron's director of communications, Craig Oliver, who I almost took as the voice of No. 10, so it was pretty much an instruction. And Thérèse Coffey rang me and said Carrie was really good, they'd worked together, and she recommended her. I may have had one or two more recommendations, but those two stick in my mind.

Whittingdale had never encountered Carrie before, but he took the advice he was given seriously.

Sir Craig Oliver, for his part, does not dispute the veracity of this story and recalls making this recommendation. '[No. 10] would occasionally deal with CCHQ and at the time of a general election we would obviously deal with CCHQ more,' he says. 'I had dealt with Carrie before. She was young and even though she wasn't very experienced she was bright and capable. It's not unusual for someone to be given the responsibility of becoming a special adviser when they're pretty young. She was obviously smart.'

Her responsibilities at this stage only went so far, however. While she would have come to David Cameron's attention in her broadcasting role, which included lining up TV and radio interviews for senior figures, she was not part of his inner circle or a regular attendee at No. 10 political meetings. Another source, who worked at the Department for Culture, Media and Sport (DCMS) at the time, claims that Carrie did seem to know Oliver quite well. 'Carrie once told me that she got Craig Oliver to parachute her into the DCMS job,' says this person. 'Originally she was going to work in another department, but she didn't want to work there and she got the DCMS job instead. I always thought she and Craig were quite pally.'

Whittingdale and Carrie soon met in his new department, which was located on the fourth floor of the Treasury building. According to him, they saw eye to eye straight away. 'I asked Carrie to come and have a chat and we got on very well,' he remembers.

> I very quickly thought we could work together well. She came strongly recommended and clearly had extremely good links with the Lobby and she'd got quite a lot of experience, working partly on campaigns. The most important thing is you have a good relationship where you can laugh together and that sort of thing. We just hit it off and I knew we would have a good working relationship. I appointed her on that basis.

Just four years after securing her first ever job in Westminster, Carrie had scaled another rung of the ladder. Now, as a temporary civil servant who was also a political appointee, she would be paid a publicly funded salary in the PB2 band. This put her earnings up to between £53,000 and £69,999, a comfortable increase on what she had been paid for working in the CCHQ press office. Moreover, she had been offered a job in a department which was considered by most people to be fun and interesting and which offered a select group of employees – of whom she was one – free access to all sorts of cultural and sporting events.

It was decided that Carrie would be Whittingdale's press adviser, though things did not exactly get off to a perfect start in her new career. It was soon noticed by Sebastian Shakespeare's *Daily Mail* diary column that she was prone to writing lowbrow messages on Twitter. These included her perception that the singer Zayn, formerly of the band One Direction, was 'too hot'. She also tweeted to her followers: 'It's getting hot in here so take off all your clothes', and delivered enthusiastic appraisals of Australian actors Guy Pearce and Eric Bana. 'Phwoar!!!!' she said of Bana, calling him 'so hot'. The account was quickly deleted. Another young woman, Mimi Macejkova, was appointed as Whittingdale's second spad at the same time as Carrie was hired. Miss Macejkova's brief was to focus on policy matters, but, to the surprise of some within DCMS, she left her post within just a few months of Whittingdale becoming Secretary of State. 'Initially, Mimi was the other spad,' explains Whittingdale.

She was good, but part of the problem is there's a spad network around Whitehall and Mimi didn't gel with the others quite in the way one hoped. I liked her, but she didn't have quite the same working relationship with officials, so after a time we reached a mutual agreement and she went to do something else and we then appointed another person in her place, Aline Nassif.

Miss Nassif, an Oxford graduate who had worked as a press officer in CCHQ for a year before joining the Department for International Development as a spad, was a friend of Carrie's, ensuring her replacement of Miss Macejkova was straightforward.

During the time that Carrie worked for Whittingdale, the BBC was probably the biggest single issue that he had to tackle in his capacity as Culture Secretary. 'We were writing a new BBC charter and she was involved in internal meetings I had,' he says. 'Obviously I was making speeches about the BBC and giving interviews, so she was helping with all of those. She had to help me with that as my media spad. She didn't have hostility for the BBC and neither did I. She followed my lead. That was her job.' Negotiating the arrangements for the governance of the state broadcaster is thought to be an occasionally tortuous process. For Carrie, though, there was always more to life than just hard work. A month into her job, at the end of June 2015, she took a mini-break to St Tropez with her friend Janna Lawrence, with whom she had been at university. Government records show that in her role as a special adviser, she accepted free tickets to a day at Wimbledon and to an Ashes game in July soon after returning from France. In between these two sporting events, she took a second short holiday, this time visiting her aunt's house in Italy. On her return, she attended lunches with Amol Rajan, then the editor of her father's former paper *The Independent*; and with Guto Harri, then the communications director of Rupert Murdoch's newspaper group, News UK. In August, she was a guest of the BBC at the Proms and shortly afterwards she went on a two-week holiday to Austria and Italy with her boyfriend, Harry Cole, who had just started a new job as Westminster correspondent at *The Sun*. The following month, she accepted tickets to see *Hamlet* at the Barbican. She was also given a pass to the iTunes Festival and tickets to a production of the play *Future Conditional* by Tamsin Oglesby, which was staged at the Old Vic.

Alongside all of these indulgences, she also bought her first flat in September 2015. It occupied the upper floor of an imposing Victorian house in Carisbrooke Road in the seaside town of St Leonards, in East Sussex. The property cost £199,000 and Carrie is known to have enjoyed scouring antiques shops to furnish it. A few days after completing the purchase, she was on duty again for DCMS, this time attending the annual ceremony for the Pride of Britain charity awards in London. There, she took a photograph of the actress Barbara Windsor and the television personality Kelly Osbourne. In between them stood the hulking figure of the then Mayor of London, Boris Johnson. Carrie posted the picture onto her Instagram account without making any comment. One friend wrote: 'My God, your life! Soooo jealous!' Without further delay, Carrie then made a short trip to the 56th Venice Biennale before heading to the Conservative Party conference, held that year in the first week of October in Manchester. This flurry of activity was capped off with an invitation to the opening night gala of the political film *Suffragette*. Unquestionably, this was a very happy and busy time in the 27-year-old Carrie's life, both personally and professionally.

Some within DCMS, however, were beginning to question privately her suitability for and commitment to the job she had been given. 'There were quite a few times when I wondered where she was and I was just told she was "off"', recalls one former colleague.

She didn't seem to come in very often and when I asked after her, I was told that she had a headache or was on holiday. She had John wrapped around her little finger. John is nice, but he obviously really wanted his job. He was so happy when he got the job. He couldn't stop talking about it. He never thought he would be a minister.

This person goes on:

Carrie had a fairly limited understanding of the job she was meant to be doing. She didn't seem to understand the structure of the party, of Parliament or of policy. I remember she was once called on to advise John on something and she asked a colleague for help and then presented it as her own work. And I never thought she was a Conservative, either. If anything, she was more like a Green or a Liberal. She wasn't very political. As a media spad you'd have thought she would be more knowledge-able about how the party worked, but she didn't seem to know anything. I don't know why she is held up as this PR guru. She did very little work. The press office did a lot of work for her when she was working for John. She came across as the nicest, sweetest person. For example, she'd claim she wanted to socialise with someone, but she had no intention of doing so. She wasn't a team player. I thought she was fake and untrustworthy. I say that as someone who tried really hard to get to know her, to see the good in her, but I couldn't. I would like to believe in the good in her, but having worked with her, it's very hard to do that. I want to be a Carrie fan, but I just can't say that I am. She is very well protected. There are many people around her who protect her. But I don't know how that came about. I do remember that she seemed to be close to some of the people in No. 10.

If Whittingdale was aware of any of these perceived shortcomings at the time, he has never said so publicly. Indeed, he remains firmly of the view that Carrie was a key part of his team who made doing his job significantly easier. 'She used to come with me to events,' he recalls.

If I was having lunch with a journalist like Allegra Stratton or with Richard Desmond, she would come with me. Anything media related, she was involved in. That included media policy. Those in the DCMS area obviously want to influence and get to know the ministers, and equally they will spend some time getting to know the spads. She was going out with Harry Cole at that time, so she had a direct link to the Lobby and she knew a lot of journalists and she had a very good network. So she was well plugged into the spad network, well plugged into No. 10 and so she was incredibly helpful in terms of keeping me informed and advising me on what was happening around government, what the spad network was talking about. She had a very good feel for the press. The press liked her. She was able to ring them up and she was very active in advising me about media bids, about where I might plant stories if we were making an announcement if we were trailing something, or about whether to go on TV or radio, and she used to come with me to media appearances. She was invaluable as a media spad. She was one of the best in her field. She was also easy-going and fun. We would frequently of an evening have a drink. She came with me on a couple of overseas trips with whatever private secretary had been allocated for that trip. You work long hours in the Cabinet. And she was having to work very long hours. We became good friends. We'd go to the pub after a hard day.

Whittingdale adds that she confided in him that her relationship with her father was not an easy one. She also told him about her experience at the hands of John Worboys. Usually, however, they spoke about work. 'She was a very strong Tory, but she was more than that,' he says.

> She came with certain strong views. Obviously at that time she was very committed to the environment and animal welfare. The only issue on which we disagreed was foxhunting. I'd voted in favour of it because I come from a very rural constituency. She was against it. She struck up a close relationship with Tracey Crouch, my Sports Minister, because Tracey was also anti-hunting, which used to annoy No. 10. Carrie was equally passionately opposed to foxhunting.

Notwithstanding Whittingdale's appreciation of Carrie's professionalism, some colleagues continued to grumble about her absences. In December 2015, she took a mid-week trip to New York for a few days, using the opportunity to visit her cousin, who owns a restaurant there. After Christmas, she attended two concerts at the Royal Festival Hall, one of which featured the pianist Daniel Barenboim. 'This job means I get to do some incredible things,' she boasted on Instagram. Having enjoyed that cultural fix, she then jetted off to Barbados for a ten-day holiday in the Sugar Bay resort. Soon after returning in February 2016, she attended the BAFTAs in

London. Later that month came the BRIT Awards ceremony. The next month she accompanied Whittingdale on an official visit to New York. And in April, she managed to squeeze in a short trip to Rome with a friend. Each of these episodes in her life, whether work-related or not, was carefully logged on her Instagram account, drawing gasps of envy from friends and slightly less enthusiastic noises from colleagues. Often, the photos she posted of the places that she visited were accompanied by a selfie, inviting further admiring observations, which were often forthcoming.

During the twelve or so months that she worked for Whittingdale, the subject that dominated British politics was, of course, the Brexit referendum. When the campaign began in earnest in February 2016, six Cabinet ministers were given permission by David Cameron to break with the government's position to remain in the EU and instead to lobby publicly to take Britain out of the bloc. The six were Iain Duncan Smith, Michael Gove, Priti Patel, Chris Grayling, Theresa Villiers and John Whittingdale. Officials were instructed that this group was not to be given access to any briefing document or other information relating to the EU for the duration of the four-month national debate. This was interpreted in different ways, depending on the department. Carrie, as someone on the civil service payroll, was also subject to certain restrictions when it came to campaigning.

'The issue that proved most difficult, and on which Carrie had strong views which were supportive of my own views, was Brexit,' Whittingdale recalls.

I was a member of David Cameron's Cabinet. At the time I was appointed, I told him I thought it unlikely I would be able to support continued membership in the referendum, and he'd said to me: 'Let me try and get a better deal,' and I'd said: 'OK.' But when I agonised a bit as to whether or not I was going to come out to join the Vote Leave campaign, she was strongly of the same mind. She suggested to me that she'd be very disappointed in me if I hadn't come out in favour of Brexit. As a spad, she was to some extent constrained in what she could do. Not only did she come with me on one or two Vote Leave meetings; she also came out during the campaign on the battle bus.

The cross-party Vote Leave campaign was based in the Westminster Tower office building near Lambeth Bridge and was run by Michael Gove's former spad Dominic Cummings. Another key figure was a former journalist, Lee Cain, who ran its broadcast unit. Both men met Carrie fleetingly during the campaign at Westminster Tower, where she is remembered to have gone with Whittingdale on occasion, but within a couple of years she would encounter them again at much closer quarters than any of them could have anticipated. 'My recollection is she would come into the office some evenings for a glass of wine and a gossip with other spads like Henry Newman and Henry Cook, who both worked for Michael Gove. Josh Grimstone was also a friend of theirs,' reports one former Vote Leave employee. 'She never actually did any work on the campaign, though. These spads hanging around used to annoy those of us who were full-time on the campaign.'

About halfway through the campaign, in April 2016, Carrie and her boss both became preoccupied by another story which had nothing to do with Brexit, nor, indeed, with politics, but which tested both of them in every sense. It concerned Whittingdale's private life. The BBC programme *Newsnight* was intending to run a story about his having had a relationship with a prostitute. Sir Craig Oliver reported in his personal account of the Brexit campaign, which was published in 2016 under the title *Unleashing Demons*, that he was rung by Carrie warning him about this delicate matter on 12 April. Oliver wrote: 'I'm almost home that evening when I get a call from … Carrie Symonds … Carrie has already drafted a statement…' The statement made clear that Whittingdale, who was divorced, had met the woman through the dating website Match. com. They had had a relationship between August 2013 and February 2014, when he was a backbench MP. He had been unaware of the woman's occupation and had ended the liaison when he discovered she was trying to expose the fact of the relationship to the press. 'This is an old story which was a bit embarrassing at the time,' the statement read. 'The events occurred long before I took up my present position and it has never had any influence on the decisions I have made as Culture Secretary.'

The BBC's principal interest in the affair apparently sprang from the fact that four newspapers – *The People*, the *Mail on Sunday*, *The Sun* and the *Independent on Sunday* – had investigated the claims and concluded that reporting the story was not in the public interest. The BBC, however, seemed to be listening carefully to campaign groups like Hacked Off, which were arguing for tighter press regulation. As Oliver describes it in his book, these campaigners had suggested that some newspapers might have used the information they had about Whittingdale's private life 'to hold a gun to his head, in case he threatened to push through the final bits of the Leveson inquiry on press regulation'. In fact, there was no evidence to support this idea at all. Still, the story dominated the news agenda for the next twenty-four hours, placing Whittingdale and, to a lesser extent, Carrie in the eye of the storm. Whittingdale has never forgotten the kindness Carrie showed him at that time. 'She was hugely helpful to me when I was the focus of media attention,' he says. No doubt others within the Conservative Party also became aware of how well Carrie had coped with this minor crisis.

Towards the end of the Brexit campaign, in June 2016, Carrie took a photo which was, as by now was standard for her, posted on her Instagram page. It showed three senior politicians boarding the infamous red bus used by the Vote Leave campaign which bore a slogan promising to spend the £350 million given to the EU each week on the NHS instead. The trio consisted of the Conservative Energy Minister, Andrea Leadsom; the Labour MP Gisela Stuart; and behind them, delivering a wave, Boris Johnson. Whittingdale says that Carrie and Johnson seemed to get to know each other slightly better during the campaign, thanks – in part – to him. 'I cannot say that I introduced her to Boris, but I don't think she knew him particularly well [before the campaign] and she will have come across him when she accompanied me to Vote Leave meetings,' Whittingdale says. This theory is backed up to some degree by Johnson himself. Whittingdale observes that when Johnson attended his 60th birthday party in early 2020, he gave a speech in which he thanked Whittingdale, saying he had helped to change the course of British political history because he was one of the six Cabinet ministers who decided to rebel against the party line and go for Brexit. 'He also said I'd changed his life in all sorts of ways, including the fact that I'd "helped bring him together with Carrie". That [Brexit campaign] would have been the first time she'd worked alongside and got to know him a bit,' Whittingdale adds.

Shortly after the result came through in the early hours of Friday 24 June 2016 that the electorate had decided by a majority of more than 1.25 million votes to leave the EU, David Cameron announced his resignation as Prime Minister. Though the full implications of the vote would take a long time to show themselves, Carrie did not seem to let the shock of these seismic events bother her. Instead, she went with friends to the Glastonbury festival for the weekend, cheerfully heedless that her own job at DCMS might be on the line depending on the identity of Cameron's successor.

The ensuing Conservative Party leadership contest, the first since 2005, was by then underway. It was swift and brutal. MPs were expected to vote in a series of ballots until only two candidates remained, at which point Conservative Party members would choose who should be their leader and, therefore, the Prime Minister. The pro-Brexit Boris Johnson was the bookmakers' short-priced favourite and to begin with he enjoyed the support of many MPs including John Whittingdale and, by association, Carrie. But on 30 June, three hours before nominations were due to close, Michael Gove moved against Johnson. The fact that Gove had up until then been assumed to be Johnson's friend, and that he was meant to be supporting him in the leadership race, ensured this political knifing has never been forgotten. 'He was spurred on to run himself by his wife, Sarah, plus his spad Henry Newman, and also by Simone Finn, his ex-girlfriend, who was then a spad as well. They convinced him,' remembers a source. On 30 June, Gove released a written statement. 'I have come, reluctantly, to the conclusion that Boris cannot provide the leadership or build the team for the task ahead,' it read. 'I have, therefore, decided to put my name forward for the leadership.' Johnson threw in the towel straight away, his longstanding ambitions dented too severely on that occasion to recover. One former colleague of Carrie's remembers this sequence of events well.

> She told me she signed up with John Whittingdale to the Boris Johnson leadership campaign in 2016. I remember talking to Gove's team at the time and asking if Michael Gove was going to run himself. I was assured he wasn't going to. The night Michael decided to shift, his team called Whittingdale, and Whittingdale – and Carrie – decided to shift with them. It's always amused me that she left Boris to join Gove.

This left five MPs to jostle for the prize: Gove, Theresa May, Andrea Leadsom, Liam Fox and Stephen Crabb. Gove's leadership campaign was chaired by Nick Boles, who had also previously backed Johnson. On 5 July, the first round of votes was cast. Fox was eliminated, having secured the backing of only sixteen MPs. Crabb also stepped away from the contest because of problems in his personal life. May, who had come top, now contested the second ballot on 7 July against Gove and Leadsom. In the second round, Gove came last with forty-six votes. Leadsom became the sole remaining pro-Brexit candidate and would face May in the final round, which was open to all Conservative Party members. Before the members had a chance to cast their votes, however, there was a further bump in the road. Leadsom gave an interview to *The Times* which was published on 9 July. In it, she was felt by some to have spoken carelessly. The view that took hold was that she was unwise to have claimed to the newspaper that her status as a mother would make her a better choice as Prime Minister than May, who is childless, because she had a 'very real stake' in the future. Secret briefings against Leadsom, together with open criticism of her, ensued. Even with uncertainty increasing as to who would be the next Prime Minister, and with growing questions over what this might mean for her own position, Carrie attended the men's Wimbledon final, where she watched Andy Murray defeat Milos Raonic. The day after, Leadsom withdrew from the leadership race. May was crowned party leader by default and on 13 July a new Prime Minister, who had voted Remain, entered Downing Street. 'Big day in Westminster today as David Cameron does his last PMQs and stands down as Prime Minister,' Carrie wrote at the time on Instagram. She added: 'Not sure I'd ever have worked for the Conservatives, had it not been for him. Feel proud to have worked for him.'

Very shortly after May's arrival, she began to appoint her new Cabinet. The shock decision to elevate Boris Johnson to the position of Foreign Secretary captured most headlines. Lower down the chain, John Whittingdale was removed as Culture Secretary and replaced by Karen Bradley, all but putting Carrie out of a job. She was sorry to see her boss go and said as much publicly on her various social media accounts, making it clear it had been a 'privilege' to work for him. Colleagues recall that Carrie had hoped to be brought into No. 10 as the new PM's head of broadcast but the job went to Tom Swarbrick, a presenter at the radio station LBC. Swarbrick was considered a clever hire. His role was to help brief May before interviews and to assist the director of communications on the government's communications strategy. According to one source, these were duties which would not have played to Carrie's strengths. 'Nobody in Downing Street wanted her to work there, either under Cameron or May. She wasn't interested enough in policy; it was that simple.'

Carrie wanted to remain in government and put the word out that she was looking for a new job. An opportunity soon arose. Salma Shah, a spad working for Sajid Javid, the newly appointed Secretary of State for Housing, Communities and Local Government (DCLG), was shortly to go on maternity leave and somebody was needed to provide six months' cover. Carrie's interest was apparently looked on favourably. A few days later, she went to France for a short break. Still officially working at DCMS, she attended a BBC Prom on her return to London. She then spent the first ten days of August holidaying in Italy. No sooner had she returned to London than she jetted off to Greece for another break. While abroad, it was confirmed that she would be joining Javid's team. 'Sajid Javid has hired Carrie Symonds as his media SpAd at DCLG,' declared the Guido Fawkes website on 22 August 2016. Showing a deference not normally accorded to every young civil servant, the website added: 'Symonds is a former Head of Broadcast at CCHQ and most recently was a spinner for Whitto at DCMS, she's well-liked in the Lobby and has a good relationship with broadcasters so is a smart hire for Saj.' This polite item failed to note that her new position was not permanent, but from early September, Carrie was based at DCLG's offices, situated within the Home Office in Marsham Street.

The business of DCLG was by its very nature in sharp contrast to that of DCMS, and Carrie might have been forgiven for feeling slightly weary at the prospect of the gear change that would be required of her in order to deal with the matters that would occupy Javid's and, by extension, her own time. These included the push to build more affordable housing; leasehold reform; brownfield site development; business rates; domestic violence; racism; and homelessness. Yet in retrospect, she might also have considered herself lucky to have secured this position. Whittingdale says he endorsed her for the post. 'Carrie went off when I lost my job,' he says. 'Theresa May and I didn't really see eye to eye, so it wasn't a huge surprise. Spads are personal appointments and they have to be because it's quite a close working relationship. I would have given her a very strong recommendation.'

Yet some within DCLG were less sure about her abilities. 'She was a bit junior and inexperienced,' recalls one member of staff.

She had been a spad for Whitto at DCMS and she'd run the broadcast desk at CCHQ in the 2015 election, so she'd done a series of junior jobs in the party, but it was felt that she lacked depth. I don't think she really understood the structural and operational requirements of her job. She wasn't interested in that stuff. Lots of spads suffer from this. They just act as bag carriers. She only ever did communications, whereas Salma did policy and comms. This gave extra work to the other spad, Nick King.

Nonetheless, she was generally considered by others in DCLG to be friendly and charming and her working relationship with Javid is said to have been as harmonious as the one she and Whittingdale enjoyed.

In September 2016, the month she began working for Javid, she sold her flat in St Leonards, exactly a year after buying it. Showing some business acumen, it achieved £269,500 on the open market, therefore delivering a profit of £70,500 excluding estate agents' fees. Having worked in DCMS until only a few weeks before, the occasional perk was still on offer to her from that source, and she seemed to embrace these opportunities. In October 2016, she wrote of having spent a 'brilliant night' with the Conservative MP and former Arts Minister Ed Vaizey at the premiere of the film *A United Kingdom* about the love affair between an African man and an Englishwoman in post-war London. It was screened at the British Film Institute, 'which this year is focussing on promoting diversity', Carrie wrote. She said it was 'even better to be there with Ed Vaizey – my old boss, friend and biggest champion of diversity in media & the arts'.

Christmas was spent with her mother and aunt in Italy and in early February 2017 she took another holiday, this time enjoying a week in the Cayman Islands. The timing of this latter trip was considered unfortunate by some at DCLG, though. 'When business rates were revalued for the first time in seven years in 2017, the *Daily Mail* ran a series of very prominent stories about how disastrous this had been for some businesses', recalls one DCLG source.

This information was released by the DCLG and Downing Street

during recess, when everybody was on holiday, which was probably one of the worst decisions that could have been made. It
should have been announced on a busy news day, because it was
not good news. And there was nobody at the DCLG thinking
about that. Carrie should perhaps have been thinking about it,
but she was posting pictures of her holiday on Instagram instead.

Things did not improve when she returned. 'The government had
to quickly introduce a small business rate relief at a cost of about
£400 million,' the source goes on.

If you're not a technical person and you're not interested in the
policy side of things and you do communications for the DCLG
during a situation like this, you would struggle. And she did. The
complexity of it went over her head. I'm really not sure she knew
whether the business rates relief was going to come from new
money or if the department was going to have to find the money
from the existing budget, in other words robbing Peter to pay
Paul. It was very amateur.

She survived the storm, and in early April she accompanied Javid
on a fact-finding trip to Finland to learn more about homelessness
prevention. At the same time in London, the political temperature
was rising, as rumours of a snap general election being called by
the new Prime Minister refused to lie down. On 18 April, Mrs May,
just nine months into her premiership, confirmed her intention
to go to the country on 8 June. Her plan was to use the poll to
shore up her position, her party by this stage having a majority of

seventeen seats in Parliament. This announcement, coinciding with the return from maternity leave of Salma Shah, brought to an end Carrie's brief tenure at DCLG.

Her spell in the department is little remembered. One source, however, says that during this period she 'spent the whole time trying to get the department to buy her a gold iPad'. This purchase, at public expense, was 'eventually approved by email from the Secretary of State's private office', according to the source, even though products made by Apple, including iPads, are understood to have been incompatible with the department's computer network at the time, making it unclear as to whether the iPad would have been able to host a DCLG email address. A Freedom of Information request was submitted to the DCLG's successor department, MHCLG, on 11 October 2021. Whereas such requests should normally be dealt with by a public body within twenty working days, this one was not answered for three months. The delay was attributed to 'public interest' reasons. The response confirmed that 'one iPad with case was purchased for a Special Adviser at a price of £538, inclusive of VAT'. The special adviser was not named. Although the request also asked to see all emails from the private office of the then Secretary of State, Sajid Javid, during this period approving the purchase of any iPads at public expense for his special advisers, this was considered exempt from disclosure on the ground that it is 'personal, about another individual' and releasing it would be in breach of UK Data Protection legislation.

Carrie's own involvement in the 2017 general campaign is noteworthy. Within a few days of May's announcement, she was canvassing and leafleting in the London area for candidates including

Gavin Barwell, the Housing Minister. Wider interest soon turned to her stamping ground of Richmond Park, however. At the point that May declared the election was on, no candidate had been adopted to fight the seat. This was in part because of recent events involving Zac Goldsmith. Having first become the area's MP in 2010, he was returned to the Commons in 2015 with a majority of 23,000. The following year, however, he resigned over the government's proposal to build a third runway at Heathrow Airport. In the ensuing by-election, in December 2016, he stood as an Independent Conservative candidate, which meant the Conservative Party decided not to field anybody against him. Against expectations, the pro-EU Liberal Democrat candidate, Sarah Olney, beat Goldsmith by 1,872 votes. This prompted Carrie to write at the time: 'My first job in politics was working for Zac Goldsmith & not sure I'd have worked for the Tories if it hadn't been for him. Owe him a lot.' Five months earlier she had written a near-identical tribute to David Cameron when he left Downing Street.

On the night of 26 April 2017, Goldsmith was hastily selected to fight the Richmond Park seat again. Carrie was on holiday in New York with a friend at the time, but when she returned to London in early May, she became part of his campaign team. Her presence was not appreciated by every other member of this small but committed group of salaried party officials and volunteers. One source close to the campaign recalls:

Zac pushed very hard to secure a paid role for Carrie on his team as some sort of communications adviser. She was between jobs at the time. When Zac asked if Carrie could have a paid job, he was told by his election agent, David Jones, that she was welcome to join us but that it would be impossible to pay her because there were no campaign funds available. I know Zac was very unhappy about that. Carrie did join, but if she was ever paid, her money certainly didn't come from campaign funds.

Morning team meetings would be held in the local Conservative Party office in the Upper Richmond Road, just around the corner from Carrie's mother's house, where she was staying at the time. Yet others who attended these meetings became frustrated at what they perceived as a lack of enthusiasm on Carrie's part for the role she had been given. 'She was utterly, utterly useless,' remembers one member of the team.

She got in the way, she swanned around and she essentially made a nuisance of herself. She basically stuck to Zac like a limpet. Wherever he went, she'd be with him. She would be in a taxi with him. She was whispering crap into his ear the entire time. A major sore point was when the council moved the arrival of postal ballots forward by several days. Zac's agent told him it was vital to react to this by getting out and knocking on doors, but Zac and Carrie had been working on a secret leaflet. They thought it would win them the seat and it was clearly their priority. I believe there was a disagreement with David Jones over that. One weekend she also went into the office and took most of the poster stock and put posters up in tiny streets where they would have had no impact. She didn't seem to have a clue what she was doing in terms of running a campaign.

There were also problems with her timekeeping. This source goes on:

> Even though she lived round the corner from the office, she was often late. There was a constant stream of excuses of why she couldn't be where she was meant to be at the right time – unless Zac was getting a taxi somewhere, and then she'd jump in the back with him. She was supposed to be in charge of comms, so she needed to be at these meetings. I would say she did little on the campaign overall compared with how hard others worked.

Foremost among those who put their back into the campaign was Goldsmith's election agent, the aforementioned David Jones. A former Army officer in his forties who was married with children, he and Goldsmith had worked together since 2013 and, though they had disagreed over tactics that had been used by Goldsmith when he tried to become Mayor of London in 2016, they are said to have had a solid working relationship. 'It was a strange campaign,' recalls a member of Goldsmith's team.

> Two weeks after Carrie turned up, David was accused by Zac of having fallen out with a younger member of the team. A show-down meeting was held in the office which several local party officials attended. Zac became increasingly irate during it. He seemed to be under pressure. He was red in the face. David, who is a very nice guy who had increased Zac's majority to over 20,000 votes at a previous election, was very hurt and confused. He denied the accusation and the same day, he walked out. There

was less than three weeks to go until polling day. He told me his position had been made impossible. It was very sad as he and Zac had been friends, but it's noteworthy, I think, that since leaving Zac in 2017 David has continued to work solidly as a Conservative Party agent in a neighbouring part of London.

In one of the last results to be declared, at about seven o'clock on the morning of 9 June, following four recounts, Goldsmith retook the seat from Olney by a margin of forty-five votes. Carrie was clearly nervous about his prospects, even ringing her former boyfriend Oliver Haiste to tell him of her fear that Goldsmith would be beaten for the second time in six months. 'I remember when Zac came back in 2017, she called me and said she thought he was going to go,' says Haiste.

Nationally, the picture for the Conservatives was disastrous. Under May's shaky stewardship, and thanks to a decidedly patchy election manifesto, the small majority she had enjoyed going into the election disintegrated. The ten Democratic Unionist Party MPs who had been returned to the Commons agreed to vote with the government, allowing May to remain in post, but the authority she had lost would never be recovered. For Carrie, however, things only improved. Richmond Park was the only constituency in London which the Tories gained during the 2017 election, and, having by then styled herself Goldsmith's 'campaign adviser', she was credited by some with having masterminded this victory. With that feather in her cap, she went on a short holiday to Germany. When she got back, she was able to announce to her friends, colleagues and contacts that she had an exciting new job which would further cement her position as a player in Westminster.

CHAPTER 6

RUCTIONS

June 2017 was a very rocky time for Theresa May. Politically wounded but limping on stubbornly, she was forced to overhaul her entire operation. These involuntary changes started at the top, with the resignations of her joint chiefs of staff, Nick Timothy and Fiona Hill. In a surprise move, Michael Gove was reinstated to the Cabinet, having spent a year in exile on the back benches. He became the new Environment Secretary. Another early appointment of the new regime was that of businessman Sir Mick Davis as chief executive of the Conservative Party. This specially created post gave Sir Mick latitude to oversee who was hired and fired. Having taken advice from a range of politicians and aides, he sanctioned Carrie being offered the job of CCHQ's director of communications, putting her in charge of the party's press and broadcast machine on an enhanced salary of about £80,000 a year. It was a big step up for somebody aged twenty-nine, but the volume of endorsements made by a host of influential figures and the lack of others applying for the post meant that Sir Mick had few options. 'Lots of people advocated that she get that job,' says one with knowledge of the situation.

> I think Robbie Gibb, who'd just been made No. 10 comms chief, backed her for it. But nobody wanted to work for Theresa at that time and there was a huge brain drain after the election. I don't think there were many people who wanted to run CCHQ's comms, put it like that.

Some of Carrie's friends in the media were quick to pat her on the back publicly after she was given this promotion. On 7 July, Guido Fawkes broke the story of her recruitment, noting that she would be 'a true Brexit believer in CCHQ' who had 'years of press experience' and who '"gets" broadcast'. This was 'another strong and much-needed Tory hire', the website added. Writing in *The Sun* a day later, political commentator James Forsyth chimed in with a further tribute, referring to her approvingly as 'the politically savvy Brexiteer'. On the day Forsyth's article appeared, Carrie put out a short message on Twitter. It read: 'Very pleased to be joining CCHQ as Director of Comms. Lots to do. Can't wait to get started.' No sooner had she made this impressive career leap than she was off on holiday, however.

Five days in Tuscany with her friend Cat Humphrey were followed by a weekend at the Secret Garden Party music festival in Cambridgeshire. Her eventual return to the office at the end of July coincided with high summer, when Parliament had broken up. In early August, she was off again, this time accompanying a group of friends to Paris for a weekend to mark the engagement of her contemporary Florence Lawes. Immediately afterwards, she spent a week in Greece. By now, even some Conservative MPs were beginning to notice the frequency with which she seemed to be away. 'Delighted you've made it to another country for a rare change,' wrote Paul Scully jokingly after she posted a photograph on Instagram of a beautiful Greek beach. 'You need to get away a bit more, Carrie,' added Nigel Adams. Undeterred, she spent the end of another week in late August in Dorset with another spad and close friend, Beth Armstrong, before journeying back to London to enjoy the Notting Hill Carnival.

In view of the major surgery that was required to repair the Tories' battered fortunes, some felt it surprising that Carrie was not more assiduous in wanting to meet the various challenges she and her new department faced head-on. One possible reason that she may not have applied herself more emphatically lay in the newly rearranged hierarchy at CCHQ, which was by this time based in offices in Matthew Parker Street, close to Parliament. Although the Tories' digital campaign was thought internally to have been efficient during the botched election, the common consensus was that the Labour Party's had been better. Sir Mick Davis concluded that the Conservatives' digital efforts must take centre stage. To that end, a bright young man called Iain Carter, who was around the same age as Carrie and who had previously worked closely with Lynton Crosby, was appointed as political director at CCHQ. Carter's brief was to run the Conservative Research Department – the hallowed training ground on which many of the party's brightest minds from Enoch Powell to George Osborne earned their spurs – as well as its digital and communications teams. Carter was, therefore, superior to Carrie, a fact which apparently never sat easily with her. Even Patrick McLoughlin, who was reaching the end of his eighteen-month tenure as party chairman at the time she rejoined CCHQ, recalls now that the pair did not always get along entirely smoothly. One former member of CCHQ staff puts it more bluntly. 'Carrie disliked Iain.' What nobody in CCHQ realised was that by the autumn of 2017, Carrie was already casting around for another job. Specifically, she approached Boris Johnson, to whom she was by then growing closer, having heard that he was looking for a new spad at the Foreign Office. To her chagrin, Johnson decided to hire Lee Cain, who had overseen Vote Leave's broadcast communications strategy, instead.

A look at Carrie's personal Twitter account from the period shows that she was happy to use it to promote a small band of senior MPs with whom she had bonded at various stages over the previous seven years just as often as she was prepared to promote the party. The principal quartet comprised Zac Goldsmith, Michael Gove, Boris Johnson and Sajid Javid. Speeches they gave, policies they espoused, observations they made and articles they favoured were trumpeted enthusiastically by Carrie. Sometimes, these covered serious issues, such as Gove's zero-tolerance approach to anybody who abused animals and his reforms to ensure better abattoir conditions. In other instances, Carrie approved of things members of this group had said. For example, on 2 August 2017, Boris Johnson tweeted from his official Foreign Secretary's account a photograph of Prince Philip, writing underneath it: 'What a fantastic servant of UK. One of the last great impregnable bastions of political incorrectness. They don't make them like that anymore.'

Carrie retweeted this, though, signalling her own rather more modern attitude to life, days later posted a photograph of two men kissing at Manchester's Gay Pride festival, one of whom was wearing a Conservative Party T-shirt, the other a Labour Party T-shirt. 'Love this,' she wrote.

Not everybody loved what she was doing in her job, or the way she was doing it, however. One former CCHQ employee remembers: 'As head of press, she was meant to be neutral and shouldn't have been spending her time promoting individuals, yet this is what she did. It annoyed people. She worked her way through Gove, Javid, Zac and Boris.' It wasn't only colleagues whose noses were put out of joint on occasion. Some Lobby journalists were also struck by the lack of help and guidance on offer from her when it came to seeking confirmation and quotes for stories involving the Conservatives. She was running a small team of press officers, and CCHQ had also hired her friend Josh Grimstone from the private sector to be head of news and broadcasting, so she should not have been expected to deal with every single query that was rung into the office personally. Yet under her authority, one political journalist who worked on a right-of-centre newspaper encountered what they perceived to be a score-settling environment in which they were repeatedly 'frozen out'. This reporter thinks this was as a result of their having previously written articles which were unhelpful to some of those who were closest to Carrie in the party, including John Whittingdale, whose affair with a prostitute had prompted press attention in 2016. 'One tactic that I can remember being used by CCHQ was not to comment on stories that we were running, no matter how many times we tried to seek a comment, and then to complain the next day that some detail or other was wrong,' says this journalist. 'It was maddening.' Other journalists were surprised at how openly critical she was of Theresa May, even taking into account the obvious tensions at the top of government as a result of Brexit. 'She actively briefed against Theresa when she did the CCHQ comms job,' says a source. 'I think it was a way of cosying up to Gove and Johnson.'

In October 2017, Carrie took some time off to travel to Morocco, staying for five nights in one of Marrakech's premier hotels, La Mamounia. Five weeks later, she travelled to America to see her friend Ben Mallett, who was studying at Yale University, and she then made for New York, where she spent several days with friends, including Cat Humphrey. Her next stop was Lebanon, where she stayed for about a week. On her return to London a few days before Christmas, it was announced that she was to become patron of the Conservative Animal Welfare Foundation, an independent organisation made up of Tory members. Michael Gove had recently heralded the government's intention to recognise animal sentience in UK law, to ban the sale of ivory, and to outlaw plastic microbeads, which are harmful to marine life. He had also vowed to oversee a 'green Brexit revolution'. Carrie's public support for each of these issues was well known, making her something of a heroine among those Tory grassroots members with an interest in animal welfare and the environment. Her appointment as a patron also suggested she was considered by some to wield influence within the party on these matters. It wasn't just Gove who was doing so much in these areas. In late October, Boris Johnson added to her steady stream of pro-environment and pro-animal welfare tweets, writing on Twitter of his pride at 'the UK's leading role in protecting the oceans'. All of this, perhaps, showed where her true policy interests lay and arguably pointed to her thinking of moving into a job outside of politics. Just after Christmas 2017, she even set up a company called The Final Straw Ltd. She was its sole director. Companies House records show that the business was to be concerned with the manufacture of cutlery. It never got off the ground and was eventually dissolved.

Around this time, her private life underwent some significant changes. Things between her and her long-term boyfriend Harry Cole had cooled off and she had become close to other men, one of whom was a married Conservative MP with a high public profile. Although I have decided not to name this individual, I can say that he was somebody other than Boris Johnson. They were even seen together in a quiet area of the House of Commons 'not quite kissing but certainly much closer than a woman would normally stand next to a male colleague, put it like that', says a source. 'The body language made it obvious something was happening.' Even still, Johnson was by then at the forefront of her mind and, for professional reasons which will become clear, they had begun to spend more time together. Indeed, another source says that in late 2017 Carrie had begun to quiz colleagues in CCHQ about his personal life. 'There was a period where she repeatedly asked about Boris, the state of his marriage and whether he was "available"', says the source.

It got to the point where it was impossible not to ask her if she and Boris had become involved. At this suggestion, Carrie once made a vomiting sign by pretending to stick her fingers down her throat. I can only think she did this either to show that she genuinely found Boris physically unattractive or just to put others off the scent.

In early January 2018, Theresa May was ready to announce a Cabinet reshuffle. This should have been an opportunity for Carrie to show off the Tories' well-oiled communications machine in all its glory and for May to reassert some of her lost authority. Yet things went awry almost before they had begun. May's weak grasp became all too evident when Jeremy Hunt, the Health Secretary, refused to become the new Business Secretary. He stayed put. Another minister, Justine Greening, was less successful in arguing her corner. She quit the Cabinet after being told she was being moved as Education Secretary to become Secretary of State for Work and Pensions. Carrie did not escape the sense of disarray. The official Conservative Party Twitter account announced – incorrectly – that the Transport Secretary Chris Grayling was to become the party chairman. The same message was sent to Tory MPs via the WhatsApp service. Just twenty-seven seconds after these messages were sent, they were deleted, yet it was too late. Hundreds of people had shared online the news of Grayling's supposed move. Subsequent coverage of the blunder published in *The Sun* stated: 'Insiders blamed the party's brand new political director Iain Carter for posting it, having fallen victim to gossip overheard from No. 10 staffers.' Other papers including the *Daily Mail* also named Carter as having been responsible for the communications error. To compound these difficulties, the Conservative Party website also collapsed, apparently because its software had not been upgraded. The reshuffle had entered the realms of farce and, whoever was responsible, some of it was down to the fact of poor communications. One source says Carrie had by then developed a reputation as someone whose trust could not always be relied upon. Colleagues believe she had a habit of briefing against other people in CCHQ, to the extent that if a disobliging story about a member of the party's staff appeared in the media, it was widely assumed that Carrie was responsible. Who leaked Carter's name to the media remains unclear, though.

In fact, it was Brandon Lewis who should have been named as the new Tory Party chairman, not Chris Grayling. On the afternoon of the reshuffle, the correction was made, and Lewis's appointment was announced. This marked a promotion from his earlier post as an Immigration Minister, and he was determined to use the opportunity to make his mark. More than that, however, Lewis's arrival is now understood to have coincided with decisions that had to be made about Carrie's own future. After Sir Mick Davis had been installed as the Conservative Party's chief executive the previous July, CCHQ had been split into two parts. Insiders say that Sir Mick ran his section like a business. He was in charge of spending and salaries and, like any good businessman, he wanted to be sure that the party was getting value for money. From January 2018, Lewis was in charge of the political side of CCHQ, and he bolstered his team by bringing back several former senior CCHQ staffers who had gone to work in the private sector, including Zoe Thorogood, Amy Fisher and Caroline Preston. 'Brandon was the new chairman and wanted to make an impact,' says one source who worked at CCHQ. 'Part of that involved changing lots of things within CCHQ, including looking at all departments and different people to see who was and wasn't performing.' According to this source, Lewis was soon made aware of concerns about Carrie's work ethic. 'A lot of people hadn't been happy about her behaviour for quite a long time. She just wasn't up to the job. She was never in the office at CCHQ. She was missing in action all the time.' It soon became clear that senior figures in CCHQ would have good reason to ask some searching questions about other aspects of Carrie's performance, not just her attendance record. Yet an issue from Carrie's past had re-emerged unexpectedly which did nothing to make any confrontation with her more straightforward.

A few days before the reshuffle, on 4 January 2018, the matter of the black cab rapist John Worboys resurfaced after it was revealed by the BBC that he was about to be released from prison. He had served ten years in custody for his crimes, including a period on remand. A Parole Board hearing about his case had been held in November 2017 and a panel had decided to approve his release with 'stringent' licence conditions, including a requirement to report to probation staff every week and a ban from contacting any of his victims. The day after the BBC's report appeared, Professor Nick Hardwick, the chairman of the Parole Board, had to apologise to any of Worboys's victims who had not been told of the decision to release him, but it was made clear that the board was under no legal obligation to explain its decision. Given the notoriety of the case, however, public outrage was immediate. Richard Scorer, a lawyer representing a group of Worboys's alleged victims whose cases had not been included in the original criminal prosecution, said they were ready to use the law to pursue Worboys if he were released.

David Gauke was appointed Justice Secretary in the reshuffle of 8 January, thrusting him into the centre of this very public row straight away. Gauke made a Commons statement in which he promised that a review into victims' involvement in the parole process would report before Easter. That vow would not contain the anger that was soon echoing around every corner of the media, however. By 13 January, the Ministry of Justice let it be known that Gauke was mulling over the possibility of a judicial review of the Parole Board's decision. On 14 January, the *Sunday Times* reported that four Cabinet ministers had 'privately warned [Gauke] that the decision to set Worboys free could be unlawful because his victims have not been consulted about the terms of his release'. Michael Gove, a former Justice Secretary, was quoted in the article, saying of Gauke: 'I'm sure he'll do the right thing.' The paper further noted that Zac Goldsmith, who was described as being the MP to two of Worboys's victims, had written to the Parole Board to point out that the failure to consult them was 'a deeply insensitive and thoughtless omission'. Goldsmith said that releasing Worboys would be 'unforgivable' and added: 'The government must now launch an urgent judicial review into the Parole Board decision.'

That day, Brandon Lewis appeared on *The Andrew Marr Show* on BBC One and was asked about the Worboys situation. Lewis said those who had suffered at Worboys's hands must be put first, arguing that if the 'advice is clear' on the possibility of a High Court challenge then 'we will look to do that'. Lewis also said:

Every victim out there, every friend and family of victims, everybody who has read about this case will want to know that we are doing everything we can to make sure that the victims are properly protected … It's absolutely right the Secretary of State for Justice will be doing everything he can to make sure this man stays behind bars.

On 17 January, the situation intensified when the chairman of the Parole Board publicly warned against 'political interference' in its decisions. Hardwick did acknowledge, though, that the board should be open to scrutiny and legal challenge, saying he would welcome any move by Gauke to seek a judicial review. That day, two of Worboys's victims launched a crowdfund appeal to raise money to legally challenge his release, asking the Parole Board not to re-lease him until the outcome of a potential second judicial review was known. Carrie soon tweeted updates to publicise the cause, which would need tens of thousands of pounds to cover legal fees. Money poured in. Then, on 19 January, it was announced by Gauke that, following legal advice, the government would not after all seek a judicial review of the Parole Board's decision because it would be unlikely to meet with success.

That weekend's newspapers were full of stories about the case. Each one made for sorry reading for the Tories, who were accused either of infighting or of being soft on crime. Most sensationally, on 21 January, the *Mail on Sunday* claimed that Michael Gove had been accused of 'knifing' Gauke, with some senior Conservatives blaming Gove for the 'furore' over the U-turn on plans to hold a ju-dicial review. 'The reversal has left Mr Gauke's reputation in tatters just two weeks after he was promoted in the reshuffle,' reported the paper, which said that Gauke was 'bounced' by Gove into challenging Worboys's release 'only for hapless Mr Gauke to be forced to rule it out'. Gove's ally Nick Boles was also mentioned in the article, where it was noted that he had lambasted Theresa May for her 'pathetic handling' of the issue. The paper further named Carrie as 'one of the key figures in the political tussle', saying that she was known to be close to Gove, had been busy online sharing articles about the case, and had retweeted a quote by Zac Goldsmith in which he claimed the decision to set the rapist free looked more and more 'grotesque'. Some felt that the lines between the personal and the political were becoming increasingly blurred in this public interest matter.

Also on 21 January, the *Sunday Times* carried a first-person piece on the Worboys attack. The article was written anonymously but was republished eight months later, on 16 September, this time unveiling the mysterious writer's identity. It was Carrie. After going through the details of her story again, she wrote:

I am genuinely terrified that [Worboys] is going to come after me. He knows where so many of his victims live. Why should we think he won't? Which comes to why I'm writing this piece. I strongly believe Worboys poses a real danger to us all. It could so easily be your mother, your wife, your sister, your daughter, your friend. I feel I would know if Worboys had raped me that night. I'd have flashbacks or there would have been horrendous tell-tale signs when I woke the next day. But I will never truly know for sure what happened after he drugged me. Many girls had similar experiences but many others were raped and know they were raped. Their lives have been blighted. We can't let that happen again.

By this point, the crowdfund appeal was gathering momentum. George Osborne and Guido Fawkes had also advertised its existence, guaranteeing even wider media coverage. Then on 26 January, Worboys's release was halted by a High Court judge, Mr Justice Supperstone, after he granted an urgent application from the women's lawyers. This meant Worboys had to remain in custody until a further hearing to decide whether the legal challenge would be allowed to go ahead. Finally, on 28 March, the decision by the Parole Board to release Worboys was quashed by the High Court. Sir Brian Leveson, Mr Justice Jay and Mr Justice Garnham ruled in favour of the two women who brought the challenge, saying that the Parole Board should have undertaken 'further inquiry into the circumstances of [Worboys's] offending'. He would have to stay in prison, where he remains to this day. Nick Hardwick resigned immediately and Gauke eventually changed the process for challenging parole decisions. Hardwick later said: 'I admire what [Carrie] did on the Worboys case a lot. I think it's a good thing he's still in prison, a good thing there's an easier way to challenge parole decisions. It took courage and skill for Carrie Symonds and the other victims to win that case.' It was certainly magnanimous of Hardwick to have taken this attitude. He did, however, sound a note of caution about whether individual cases might start to have a disproportionate impact on criminal justice policy.

He was not the only one to have reservations. Some in West-minster believed that no matter how justified she had been in campaigning to keep Worboys locked up, Carrie had shown herself to be overtly political rather than working in the interests of the Conservative Party. The publicity effort she embarked on to keep Worboys behind bars was admired, but her activities in promoting the crowdfunding after the Conservative government's decision not to seek a judicial review of the Worboys case was considered to be akin to a breach of protocol. 'The Worboys thing is quite interesting because she basically campaigned against the government from CCHQ,' says a former senior party official.

I'm not sure how it was seen, but that was the fact. The government was basically going along with the Parole Board, and she led the campaign for the petition. Which I think is excellent, and well done her, but it is a strange dynamic. But she was right. That is actually a testament to her character, I think. It takes a toughness to do that and a determination. And skill as well, because it was quite a significant campaign, and she did that.

By the time the High Court decided Worboys would remain in prison, Carrie had become involved in an entirely separate legal action which warrants scrutiny. This second legal case involved Richard Holden, a former colleague of Carrie's who had worked with her in the CCHQ press office several years before. In February 2017, Holden had been forced to resign as an aide to the then Defence Secretary Michael Fallon after being accused of groping a woman at a Christmas party in December 2016. His resignation and the sex assault claim were leaked to the BuzzFeed news website in November 2017. In May 2018, Holden's case was heard at Southwark Crown Court. There, it emerged that the alleged victim had not complained to anyone about the alleged sexual assault for nearly two months. Then, she had told Carrie about it. At that time, Carrie was working as a spad to Sajid Javid at DCLG. Javid was also told about it and said the police should be informed.

The court heard that the alleged victim said she had not reported the alleged incident sooner because she 'didn't realise it was a crime … This was just a thing that happened at a party.' The alleged victim also said that a friend had encouraged her to come forward to prevent it happening to other women. She had also informed Anne Milton, the Tory Deputy Chief Whip. The alleged victim further explained in court that one of Holden's hands 'went down behind my skirt and between my tights and underwear'. Holden denied the allegations. His former boss Baroness Stowell, the ex-Leader of the House of Lords, was among those to give evidence on his behalf.

Carrie and Sajid Javid – who had become Home Secretary by the time the case went to court in May 2018 – both gave evidence in support of the alleged victim. A written statement by Carrie was read out to the court. In his evidence, Javid said that a Conservative official had told him that Holden 'grabbed [the] backside bare flesh' of the alleged victim 'hard'. He added that 'no one' saw this. It was considered pretty remarkable that a Home Secretary should be giving evidence in a court case of this nature seeing as he had not been at the party in question. What was more remarkable, however, was that – ironically – the evidence he gave helped to guarantee

Holden's innocence, because it clashed with the account the alleged victim had given to the court.

Holden had been charged with sexual assault by touching the alleged victim's clothes, not her skin, as Javid said the woman had told him. Javid's evidence also appeared to contradict the alleged victim's account that she had told him nobody had heard the incident, for she told the court someone 'screamed "get off or fuck off!"' and pulled Holden off her physically. In an unexpected turn of events, Holden's legal team said they accepted Javid's statement as a factual account of what the woman had told him, but they claimed that she had contradicted it in court, undermining her own credibility. After a five-day trial, it took less than thirty minutes for a jury to clear Holden. Judge Deborah Taylor told him he left the court 'without a stain on his character'. After the verdict, Holden said he had been through a 'Kafkaesque living nightmare' which cost him £150,000 in legal fees and lost earnings. He did, however, manage to rebuild his life and has been the Conservative MP for North West Durham since 2019. Javid has never commented publicly on his role in the trial.

Both of these high-profile cases took place at the very time that the chief executive of the Conservative Party, Sir Mick Davis, and others within CCHQ were attempting to understand more about Carrie's modus operandi at work, meaning the issues became fused to some degree. One source says: 'Because of the Worboys stuff, which was going on at the same time, her name was in the paper quite a bit. HR had to be very careful of that. There was a duty of care issue that had to be recognised. It became more complicated.' Some of Carrie's friends in high places also took an interest in what was going on. This did not make the task of finding out whether she had behaved in a questionable manner in relation to her work at CCHQ any easier. 'Zac and Sajid contacted Brandon Lewis and asked him not to get rid of Carrie,' remembers one source. 'They lobbied for her to stay.'

Yet Lewis alone was not involved in deciding her future. Sir Mick Davis was the prime mover. He was aware of two principal areas of concern. The first was her commitment to her job as director of communications; the second related to the amount of expenditure she had incurred in the form of taxi journeys which had ultimately been charged to CCHQ. Under a longstanding arrangement, CCHQ had an account with a minicab firm. Taxis could be booked by staff using a password. The name of whoever made the booking would be logged by the firm. It transpired that some journeys had been booked by Carrie for use in her private time. Not only that, but these bookings had been made using the names of junior members of staff without their knowledge to disguise the fact that they were for her. A certain amount of detective work was required to establish this. A former CCHQ employee says: 'Someone looked at the figures and said, "Why is so-and-so spending all this cash on taxis?" That's how it came out.'

During the inquest into the taxi bills, the name of one junior press officer, Harriet Smith, cropped up more often than any other. Miss Smith, who is described as 'very sweet and rather shy but the most hard-working press officer in CCHQ at the time', is the goddaughter of two well-known Tory Party figures: the ex-MP and now *Times* columnist Matthew Parris, and Patrick (now Lord)

McLoughlin, who was the party chairman during some of the time that the taxi bills were run up. The source says they cannot rule out the possibility that she was considered 'easy pickings' by Carrie. 'Carrie is ultra-confident in a way that Harriet is not,' says this person. 'Carrie was awful to her. Not only that, but I do wonder if her status as the goddaughter of the party chairman was thought [by Carrie] to provide some cover if this ever became an issue. Harriet was extremely upset about the whole thing.'

The political fallout from Brexit overshadowed Theresa May's premiership, and Boris Johnson was one of May's fiercest critics. Yet sources who worked in CCHQ at the time say it is highly relevant to point out that nobody there knew that Carrie had recently struck up a relationship with Johnson when these matters were tackled in the first half of 2018. The fact of her affair with Johnson was known only by a small number of people, as shall become clear in the next chapter. 'Problems about Carrie had been brewing for some time,' says one source.

It was becoming clear things weren't really fixable. This didn't happen overnight. Issues had been cropping up for a long time. The problem for Sir Mick Davis was it happened on his watch. No one had any idea she was seeing Boris at the time. Those rumours started months after. So it wasn't a political decision [to challenge Carrie], which maybe she felt it was. It was purely down to performance and expenditure. In any job, if you're not performing, you can't expect to stay. If someone stops showing up to the office regularly, you can only defend that behaviour for a certain period of time. She didn't appear to be enjoying the job. She just wanted to be in Westminster or out gallivanting. She lived in places like Annabel's and 5 Hertford Street.

Carrie's predilection for peppering her social media accounts with bulletins of where in the world she was at any given time had, seemingly, begun to catch up with her. It became impossible to ignore. 'The absence issue was quite something,' says another source.

> We all got the same amount of annual leave – twenty-five days – and her social media was looked at. It was very clear that she was off more than she should have been. And she was earning a decent salary. It was about £80,000. That was very good for someone of her age and experience, which was limited actually to CCHQ and some spad jobs. She had very little employment experience outside Westminster.

The source adds: 'Mick soon realised her appointment had been an error and she was the wrong choice.'

Throughout the first half of 2018, Carrie continued life much in the way she had always done, in spite of the ongoing questions at work. She attended the Cheltenham Festival with her CCHQ colleague Josh Grimstone and journalist Alex Wickham, who by then was among her closest male friends. Two parties were held to celebrate her 30th birthday. The first was in Soho with Grimstone, Wickham, Cat Humphrey and another CCHQ colleague who had recently been hired to work in the press office, Sophia True. Miss True is the daughter of another Tory peer, Lord True.

The second party took place at the London house of Simone Finn, Michael Gove's former spad, who had by then set up a political consultancy with the ex-Tory minister Francis Maude. Demonstrating the regard in which Carrie was held by top political figures by this point, the party was attended by several Cabinet ministers, including Javid, Gove and Johnson. Carrie's favourite band, ABBA, played on the stereo for most of the night and she was seen dancing with Johnson. The music was only switched off to make way for Gove. He drew attention to himself by performing a rap seemingly in praise of Johnson, who was said to have been 'perplexed' by the performance. Looking back on that event, several Conservative Party sources are themselves still flummoxed. One says: 'It's not normal for a young woman to have that many middle-aged male Cabinet ministers at her 30th birthday. It's weird.'

In early May, the local elections took place, requiring Carrie's professional attention. Immediately afterwards, however, she went on holiday to Portugal for a week with her university friend Janna Lawrence. Having arrived back in London, she announced that she was off straight away on a 'birthday trip' to Morocco, in the middle of the working week, with Josh Grimstone and Sophia True. As all three of them worked in the CCHQ press office, this reportedly left it understaffed, angering party chiefs.

Due to the fact that a non-disclosure agreement was eventually signed between Carrie and CCHQ, it is unclear precisely when and why the situation exploded, but it did. That Carrie is said to have spent thousands of pounds on taxis using other people's names cannot have helped matters. One former colleague subsequently told the *Daily Mail*: 'It came to a head when someone questioned why junior staff were taking so many cabs, including late at night and at weekends. The junior staff didn't know and were worried they would get into trouble.' Other former colleagues remain deeply unimpressed by the episode to this day. One says: 'She's lucky she didn't end up in more serious trouble. I think it's only because of where she worked that nobody wanted to draw more attention to it. It was misuse of CCHQ funds. She used the names of those just starting out on their careers. That was unforgivable.' The affair also had implications for CCHQ at a corporate level. In particular, it would have made for a certain amount of awkwardness between Johnson and party chief executive Sir Mick Davis. Not a word was leaked to the press at the time about her being forced to quit.

Despite all of this turbulence, Carrie does not in any way appear to have been knocked off course. In June she went to America for about a week with her friend Cat Humphrey. The next month, she completed a £675,000 deal to buy a two-bedroom flat next to Brunswick Park in Camberwell, moving in there with Cat Humphrey as her flatmate. Then, on 2 August 2018, the Guido Fawkes website reported what it called 'a raft of major departures from CCHQ and Number 10'. At the top of the list was Carrie's change in circumstances. 'Tory party Director of Communications Carrie Symonds is leaving CCHQ after 8 years working for the party and in government,' the item revealed.

A true green Tory, as anyone who follows her on Twitter has no doubt gathered, she is off to work in ocean conservation. Guido hears Symonds has been snapped up by Bloomberg to lead on their Vibrant Oceans Initiative at the Commonwealth Secretariat.

Symonds will be a significant loss for CCHQ, popular with MPs and the Lobby, she has massively improved the place since coming back after the election. Congratulations.

On this occasion, Guido Fawkes's reporting was not quite accurate. Carrie was not going to work for Bloomberg, the well-known media company owned by former New York Mayor Michael Bloomberg. Rather, she was going to work for its charitable arm, Bloomberg Philanthropies. There is a key difference. Some senior figures within Bloomberg saw straight away that this error ought to be corrected. They wanted it to be clarified. 'They were really unhappy about that and were trying to find out what they could do to amend it without causing a fuss,' remembers one source. 'But when it came out soon afterwards that she was with Boris, they dropped it.' It was almost as though Carrie was becoming untouchable.

CHAPTER 7

THE BEGINNING OF THE AFFAIR

In early 2018, Carrie respectively cemented and began new relationships with two very different people, both of whom, she says, have had a profound effect on her life. The first of these was Boris Johnson, to whom she had not become close until that point; the second was her friend Nimco Ali, who came to Britain as an asylum seeker more than thirty years ago. Carrie had never met Miss Ali before 2018. It says something about Carrie's personality and character that she should have become linked so intensely with two people of such contrasting backgrounds in such a short space of time.

Johnson and Carrie had begun seeing more of each other from late 2017. Having failed to persuade him to employ her as his special adviser at the Foreign Office that autumn, she offered to give him personal advice on his media strategy. By then, many people in the Conservative Party had concluded that Theresa May's tenure in Downing Street would be more short-lived than she was perhaps prepared to accept. Johnson was among them. He believed that his public persona and proven success as a two-time Mayor of London made him the strongest candidate to replace her. Carrie bought into this idea as well, and she was an early member of the campaign team which he put in place for his second tilt at the leadership in the space of three years.

In the meantime, he remained at the Foreign Office, but he was not having an easy time there. Having played a leading role in the Brexit referendum campaign, he was not popular with everybody in this broadly pro-EU government department. Staff at all levels questioned his commitment to his brief and he was widely mistrusted. Many thought he was quite simply the wrong politician to represent Britain's interests abroad. As Foreign Secretary, however, he did have around him a small number of allies on whom he could depend. They included his team of principal advisers: David (now Lord) Frost; Lee Cain, his media spad; and Ben Gascoigne, another adviser who had first worked for him in City Hall and who knew him and his family well. In late 2017, some within the Foreign Office began to tell Johnson that the sheer volume of work that had to be done by them in this semi-hostile environment – exacerbated by the uncertainties of Brexit – meant that he should hire a chief of staff. Installing somebody of the highest competence in this post would, they believed, ease their collective burden. This suggestion seemed to fall on deaf ears.

Then, in early 2018, Johnson became keener on this plan. He soon began mentioning Carrie as a possible candidate for the plum job, which would command a six-figure salary and come with significant responsibility. His allies were 'aghast', according to one source. Even those who did not know Carrie personally knew enough about her career to have formed the view that somebody of her relative inexperience had been lucky to secure her job as director of communications at CCHQ. A senior post at the Foreign Office would have placed her out of her depth, they felt, with potentially disastrous consequences. 'Everyone advised him not to do it,' says a source. 'They told him she had been over-promoted and that making her his chief of staff was ridiculous.' No more was said about it.

One afternoon during the working week in the early spring of 2018, a Conservative MP who was used to dropping into Johnson's parliamentary office without warning walked in abruptly, as was his custom. He found Johnson and Carrie in what has been described as 'a compromising situation'. The MP, whose identity I know but whom I have decided not to name, confided in one of Johnson's closest allies about his delicate discovery. That person then told two members of Johnson's staff at the Foreign Office. One member of the quartet who was privy to this awkward secret was dismayed that Johnson had betrayed his wife, Marina, whom he knew and liked. Others took the view that it was none of their business. All suddenly understood why Johnson had been so keen to hire Carrie as his chief of staff. Knowing of his habit of compartmentalising different areas of his life, none of the four people who knew about it discussed with him at the time his latest adulterous relationship. One of them did reveal the incident when being interviewed for the purposes of this book, however.

Unaware that his core team knew of his new love interest, Johnson returned once more to floating the idea of Carrie becoming his new chief of staff. This time he tried a new tactic, invoking the name of a third-party endorser. 'I remember he said that Zac Goldsmith had told him Carrie would be brilliant in that role,' recalls one who was close to the situation. Ben Gascoigne threatened to resign if Carrie were hired. This seemed to send a clear signal to Johnson that it was a bad idea, and the scheme was kicked very firmly into touch.

His relationship with Carrie was still largely unknown by this point, but, looking back, there were some tell-tale signs of the dalliance. There is a photograph that was taken outside the Natural History Museum in early February 2018, on the night of the Conservative Party's Black and White fundraising ball, which has been reproduced in newspapers many times since. It shows the couple standing together with broad, if slightly guilty-looking, smiles. And it is also now known that a few days after that picture was taken, the pair had a Valentine's Day meal at Rules, reputedly London's oldest restaurant and, coincidentally, the venue of the first liaison between the lead characters at the heart of Graham Greene's Catholic novel about an extramarital relationship, *The End of the Affair*. As Carrie and Johnson are keen readers who were both also baptised as Catholics, this fact might not have been lost on them.

As Theresa May's premiership continued to teeter that spring, Johnson was holding regular secret meetings about his own leadership plans. These usually took place in his official London residence, 1 Carlton Gardens, with only his closest allies present. Among them was Munira Mirza, who had been his adviser when he was Mayor; Dominic Cummings, who had by then moved into the private sector; and Lee Cain. His wife, Marina, a highly rated barrister who had been the voice of reason throughout their 25-year

Carrie and her mother, Josephine, have always
been close. Carrie's ex-boyfriend Oliver Haiste says:
'[In effect] Carrie had no grandparents, siblings
or father. Her life was very mother-centric.'

Despite being married, Hilda Harrisson, Carrie's
paternal great-grandmother, struck up a close friendship
with the Liberal Party Prime Minister H. H. Asquith
after they met playing bridge in 1915. Rumours persist
to this day that they had an affair which led to the birth
of Anne Harrisson, Carrie's grandmother. If true, this
would mean Carrie is Asquith's great-granddaughter.

LEFT Carrie's complicated family tree includes the left-wing journalist and politician Lord Ardwick. His extramarital affair with Carrie's grandmother, divorcee Anne Symonds (née Harrisson), led to the birth of Carrie's father, Matthew. Although Ardwick was Carrie's grandfather, one source says he had 'almost nothing' to do with her before he died in 1994.
© Photoshot/TopFoto

BELOW Carrie's paternal grandmother, Anne Symonds (pictured with Tory grandee Reginald Maudling in 1964), was a successful BBC radio presenter who was friendly with many politicians of her era including Enoch Powell and Denis Healey. She died aged 100 in 2017. © BBC

Carrie's father, Matthew Symonds (right), founded *The Independent* in 1986 with Andreas Whittam Smith (left) and Stephen Glover (centre). His extramarital affair with Carrie's mother, an *Independent* lawyer, resulted in Carrie's birth in 1988. He paid Carrie's school fees, but she remained an adjunct to his family.
© Jane Bown/Guardian News and Media

At Warwick University, Carrie performed in plays including this one about the occultist Aleister Crowley. Before university she apparently auditioned for a part in the Hollywood film *Atonement*, but her ambition to be a professional actress was abandoned early. She is still said to be able to shed tears on cue. © Politicalite.com

Carrie canvassing with Zac Goldsmith in his Richmond Park constituency. He kickstarted her career in politics by employing her as a junior aide in 2010 and has helped her in a variety of ways ever since. After Goldsmith lost his seat in 2019, Boris Johnson gave him a peerage.
© Jeremy Selwyn/Evening Standard/eyevine

Carrie's penchant for travel and holidays did not go unnoticed among MPs or party chiefs when she worked in CCHQ. The frequency of her trips once prompted one MP, Nigel Adams, to tell her sarcastically: 'You need to get away a bit more, Carrie.'

An eye on the future? Carrie worked on Boris Johnson's 2012 London mayoral bid, but they did not have much to do with each other during it. He was more interested in Jennifer Arcuri at the time.
© Avalon.Red

John Whittingdale, for whom Carrie acted as a special adviser in 2015–16, says she was brilliant at her job and he remains a firm friend of hers. In 2020, Whittingdale was credited by Boris Johnson with having brought him and Carrie together. © David Hartley

Carrie's fondness for posting photographs of herself on social media has often attracted attention. One friend says that as a student she sent a picture of herself to the men's magazine *FHM*, which was running a competition called High Street Honeys.

Two of Carrie's closest friends in politics are Simone Finn and Henry Newman. Both were given top jobs in Downing Street after Johnson's chief adviser Dominic Cummings left in November 2020, fuelling the idea that she created a court around herself.

Two of Carrie's ex-bosses are Zac Goldsmith and Sajid Javid. One source says when she worked as Javid's adviser, she 'spent the whole time' trying to get his department to buy her a gold-coloured iPad. An FoI response shows this item was bought with public money for £538, but the recipient was not named.

Carrie's occasional bursts of exuberance have sometimes prompted comment. Here, she is seen dancing on the bonnet of a car parked in Westminster. One friend says: 'She's always been an attention seeker.'

Carrie and her future husband were photographed together outside the Conservative Party's Black and White Ball in London in February 2018. The following week, they were spotted on Valentine's Day at the London restaurant Rules. Soon after, Johnson's wife, Marina Wheeler, announced she wanted a divorce. © Ben Cawthra/LNP

Stanley Johnson made his first public appearance with Carrie in London in January 2019 at a protest against Japanese whaling. Their shared enthusiasm for animal rights and environmental matters has helped them to form a bond. © John Stillwell/PA Archive/PA Images/Alamy Stock Photo

Carrie arriving at Johnson's Tory leadership campaign launch in June 2019 with her friend Nimco Ali. A source says she claimed to hate press attention 'but she seemed to do all that she could to be centre stage'. Another source says she 'interfered' throughout the 'nightmare' campaign. © Peter Macdiarmid/LNP

After police were called to Carrie's flat in June 2019 following a now infamous row between her and Johnson, this photo was given to the press. Although billed as the first time they had been pictured together since the row, many thought it was staged. Others suggested it was an old photograph taken before the row.

The behaviour of Dilyn, a rescue dog from Wales, has caused debate and discussion since his arrival at Downing Street in September 2019. When *The Times* claimed he was to be rehomed, one source says Carrie 'freaked'. Remarkably, all reference to that *Times* story has been expunged from its records.

© Stefan Rousseau/PA Archive/PA Images/Alamy Stock Photo

In December 2019, Johnson's party won an eighty-seat majority, crushing Labour. When a colleague of Dominic Cummings had a congratulatory chat with him after the result came through, Cummings said: 'This is a disaster. Watch Carrie go to work on [Boris] now. I give it six months before we're out of a job.' In fact, Cummings lasted eleven months, leaving Downing Street in November 2020.

© Henry Nicholls/Reuters/Alamy Stock Photo

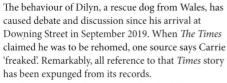

Concerns have been raised in No. 10 about Boris Johnson's relaxed attitude to official matters. This includes who has had access to highly classified material in his red boxes, necessitating a security review.

© Yui Mok/PA Images/Alamy Stock Photo

Carrie posted this picture on Instagram in February 2020, saying: 'We got engaged at the end of last year … and we've got a baby hatching early summer.' This made Johnson the first Prime Minister to have got divorced and married in office since the Duke of Grafton in 1769.

Their secret wedding in May 2021 made Johnson the first Prime Minister to marry in office since Lord Liverpool married Mary Chester in 1822. Covid restrictions meant only thirty guests attended.

© Rebecca Fulton/Downing Street via Getty Images

Rachel Johnson accompanies her sister-in-law and brother to Carrie's LGBT rights speech at the Conservative Party conference, 2021. Rachel had still not met Carrie almost two years after the latter's relationship with Boris Johnson began, leading to the idea that their own friendship is only lukewarm.

© Christopher Furlong/Getty Images

marriage, would also attend periodically. The conclusion of these talks was always the same: he had to resign as Foreign Secretary before any challenge to Theresa May could be mounted. 'He dithered for a long time,' says one who knows him well. 'He wanted to succeed Theresa May and he knew that he could, but he dithered.'

The benefits of high office, such as his ministerial car, his official residence in London and his exclusive access to Chevening House in Kent – together with the opportunities for travel he enjoyed – are said to have played their part in ensuring he stayed onside until a crucial Cabinet meeting held at Chequers on 6 July. This meeting was supposed to determine the future relationship between the UK and the EU and resulted in the emergence of the Chequers plan, a proposal covering economic, security and institutional arrangements. It was written off by many ministers straight away. They thought it would keep Britain tied too closely to the EU for all practical purposes. Within forty-eight hours of its emergence, the Brexit Secretary, David Davis, and the Brexit Minister, Steve Baker, had resigned. On 9 July, Johnson followed suit.

His eventual decision to quit the Cabinet coincided with the breakdown of his marriage becoming public. By then, Marina had found out about his affair with Carrie, whose own trials and tribulations meant that she was shortly to leave her job at CCHQ, as detailed in the previous chapter. Indeed, the affair was beginning to become known, thanks in no small part to the fact that the police protection officers to which he was entitled as Foreign Secretary were with him all the time. Gossip was inevitable. The married couple rowed, as they had done several times before because of his straying. Any hope that Marina might forgive this latest transgression was soon put to rest, however. For Marina, Carrie is said to have represented the final humiliation. Johnson's infidelities had caused her and their four children much heartache over the years. In 2009, he had even fathered a daughter with another woman, Helen Macintyre. Marina told friends that she could take no more and she wanted to divorce. Johnson is said to have been stunned.

The generational difference between him and Carrie did not escape the attention of Marina's friends. They observed that he was old enough to be her father and struggled to see what the couple could have in common. (In fact, being twenty-four years Carrie's senior, Johnson is closer in age to her mother, Josephine, who is seventeen years older than him.) What goes on between any married couple, especially one in the throes of an acrimonious separation, can be difficult for others to decipher. But one who knows about the situation says: 'For Boris, Carrie was a fling. He never expected to be with her long-term. He was shocked when Marina said she was divorcing him. He never expected it. So he settled for Carrie.' Another unpleasant reality for him to accept was the reaction of his and Marina's children, who are close in age to Carrie. They sided with their mother.

Although he was no longer Foreign Secretary, Johnson stayed put in the official residence at Carlton Gardens that he had occupied since 2016, living there rent-free. This was a breach of protocol and Sir Simon McDonald, the Permanent Secretary at the Foreign Office, wrote to him several times asking him to leave. Luckily for Johnson, his successor as Foreign Secretary, Jeremy Hunt, showed understanding of his self-inflicted predicament and did not force the issue. When Johnson did belatedly vacate the property, on 30 July, he headed for his family's country house near Thame in Oxford-shire. There, he continued to plot his future, also using his freedom as a backbencher to re-enter into his £275,000-a-year contract to write a weekly column for the *Daily Telegraph*. The money was no doubt welcome, but arguably the publicity which this refuge was capable of generating was just as important to him given that his sights were now set on 10 Downing Street. One of his earliest ef-forts for the *Telegraph* was a piece about niqabs and burkas which appeared on 6 August. Denmark had recently banned the wearing of these items in certain settings. Although Johnson argued against the ban, he did state that he thought it 'absolutely ridiculous' that Muslim women 'should choose to go around looking like letter boxes' or 'bank robbers'. This provocative language generated uproar in some quarters, but it was guaranteed to ensure that he eclipsed, albeit temporarily, the profile of the increasingly exhaust-ed Theresa May.

That August, Carrie spent the first two weeks of her new life out-side CCHQ in Italy, staying with her aunt and other family mem-bers. On her return, she felt at liberty to be even more open about her new relationship than she had been previously. It would only be a question of time before newspaper reporters knew enough about the situation to write about it, and there was a growing list of clues for them to go on. Earlier in the summer, for example, it did not go unnoticed that she and Johnson had arrived within a minute of each other at a *Spectator* party held in Old Queen Street. One who was present says: 'I remember thinking it was intriguing. I thought to myself, "Why is she here?"' Perhaps it was a sense of certainty that others would eventually cotton on to the relationship that emboldened Carrie to focus her interest on her boyfriend's political career. One who was close to Johnson at the time recalls:

That summer, she tried to muscle in. She badmouthed some of his staff and tried to persuade him that he needed to hire new people on his team. She invited Alex Wickham and Ross Kempsell, who had both recently left Guido Fawkes, to Thame to play tennis with Boris. He didn't listen to her and they were never hired.

In late August, Johnson took his four children to his father Stanley's holiday villa on Greece's Pelion peninsula. Marina is understood not to have been with them. It so happened that Carrie was in Greece at the same time, though she and Johnson are not known to have met. Then, on 7 September, *The Sun* broke the news of his marital problems. 'Bonking Boris Booted Out By Wife' roared the front-page story. His daughter Lara was quoted in the article. 'Fashion journalist Lara, 25, is understood to have been overheard exploding with rage at her philandering dad,' the paper reported. 'She is said to have told pals at a party he "is a selfish bastard". And she insisted to one friend: "Mum is finished with him. She will never take him back now."' Carrie's name did not feature in the copy, which was written by the then political editor of *The Sun*, Tom Newton Dunn, though it was noted that 'rumours had circulated in Westminster that Boris had started to give his police protection officers the slip for illicit liaisons while he was Foreign Secretary'.

The next day, Johnson went with his son Milo to the Oval to watch England's final Test against India. Sitting on his own at one point, he was looking down at his phone when the television cameras spotted him in the crowd. When his face flashed onto the big screen in the ground, a chorus of boos rose from the stands. This antagonism reflected the results of an opinion poll published that day which suggested the breakdown of his marriage could make it harder for the Conservatives to win the next election if he were party leader. While 21 per cent of voters said they would be more likely to vote for the Tories with Johnson in charge, 30 per cent said they would be less likely.

On 9 September, a second article by Johnson which used what might be described as goading language was published, this time in the *Mail on Sunday*. In it, he attacked Theresa May's Brexit plan, saying she had 'wrapped a suicide vest' around the British constitution and 'handed the detonator' to Brussels. His detractors in the Tory Party accused him of using this metaphor to try to deflect attention away from his personal life. By then, he and Marina had released a joint statement confirming that they had separated 'some time ago' and were in the process of getting a divorce. But whatever he had written that day was overshadowed by further coverage of his private life in the *Sun on Sunday*, which named Carrie as the new woman in his life. 'The former Foreign Secretary has been texting her at all hours and once sent his car to pick her up at a wedding,' the paper revealed. 'His wife is understood to have found a string of text messages between the pair.' One source told the paper that the affair had been going on for several months. 'It's fair to say they've grown incredibly close and there is a real bond of trust and friendship between them,' this person told the paper. It was claimed they had gone to 'extraordinary lengths' to meet 'during and after work'. This included his escaping official engagements to attend her 30th birthday party and 'bombarding' her with text messages 'which she sometimes delighted in showing friends'. An unnamed Tory MP added: 'About a month ago, I was at a private get-together for Leavers, where we were deciding what to do next. Boris arrived with Carrie. They seemed inseparable and spent most of the evening chatting to each other before leaving together. They looked very close.' The *Mail on Sunday* also identified Carrie that day, publishing a recent night-time photograph of her standing, arms aloft, in a pair of shorts and a T-shirt on the bonnet of a car parked outside the Palace of Westminster. Like so many aspects of her life, it had been posted on Instagram.

Although Carrie had become involved with Johnson willingly, none of this can have been easy for her. Some people point out that she perhaps failed to comprehend fully how blinding the glare of publicity would be once the truth of the affair was exposed. As soon as she was named, every newspaper wanted to know as much about her as possible. And not every portrait that appeared was entirely flattering. On 10 September, for example, *The Times* quoted an unnamed source as saying:

She was one of these girls who would be at all the parties. I can't remember her doing any work that was really good but she was always at every party going. The Tories love a social gathering and there were always a lot of parties for her to be at. The rest of us always wondered how she could afford all the dresses and designer handbags and the going out, on her kind of salary. Her friends were all beautiful. It looked like an episode of *Love Island*. But she didn't blow away any of us at No. 10.

It was not lost on Westminster observers that while affairs are not uncommon, it is often the single woman – rather than the married man – who gets the bigger share of the blame.

Realising that Johnson's political future might be compromised by the affair becoming common knowledge, the couple decided to take advice to help them steer their way through the media onslaught. 'When Carrie and Boris's relationship was developing, and intense media scrutiny was increasing to the extent that Carrie couldn't open the door of her flat without banks of cameras being there, I know that they turned to someone who has operated in the media for help,' says a friend. 'They didn't know anyone else with that sort of expertise and knowledge. She talked to them about how and when the relationship would become public.'

Awkwardly, Carrie was due to begin her new job on 10 September. The start date had to be renegotiated while she took cover for a few days. As previously noted, the job was linked to Bloomberg, but it had nothing to do with the media company itself. In fact, she was going to work for an organisation called Oceana, which protects and restores oceans and to which Bloomberg's philanthropic arm has given significant sums of money. Little was known about how this career opportunity came about until October 2020. It was then that it came to light that the Goldsmith family had, once again, been instrumental in guiding her. This emerged when Zac Goldsmith's younger brother, Ben, admitted that he had lent a hand. He gave a long interview to *The Times* about a series of matters which had nothing to do with either Carrie or Johnson. At the end of the interview, which was conducted by Charlotte Edwardes, it was noted that 'the only time he [Ben] becomes uncomfortable' was when he was asked about Carrie. He explained that Carrie was more [Zac's] friend than his. 'I was one of the people that she consulted, and I introduced her to the Bloomberg Philanthropies people,' he told the newspaper. 'She ended up securing a job with them. And then they seconded her to Oceana, which is where I think she still works. In terms of social occasions, I've probably only met her once.' Ben Goldsmith was the third member of his family, after his cousin Zeno and brother Zac, to have acted in Carrie's interests to such great effect.

The media storm and accompanying interference in Carrie's day-to-day life that her relationship with Johnson caused her at this point does lead quite naturally to trying to understand better what it was about him that attracted a woman of her capabilities. Although power is often cited as being an aphrodisiac, Johnson was on the back benches by this stage, with no guarantee that he would ever make it to Downing Street. Yet Carrie seemed happy to stand by him. Many will wonder why, especially given that a significant age gap between any couple very often fails to mask differences in outlook and temperament. One of Johnson's former lovers, Petronella Wyatt, with whom he formed an extramarital relationship in the early 2000s, can be said to have known him as well as anybody in his adult life. Indeed, they remained in touch until comparatively recently. Miss Wyatt says that even now, twenty years after he became a well-known public figure, many people misunderstand him and perhaps overlook his fragility, which dates back to the traumatic childhood he suffered. When he was ten, his mother, Charlotte, had a nervous breakdown and was committed to the Maudsley Hospital in London for nine months with depression. His parents' marriage was turbulent and they later divorced.

'He was shy when I first met him,' says Wyatt.

He wrote poetry, some of it in Greek, and seemed almost frightened of women. He had no female friends. He was solicitous. We would have long lunches and talk about history. And we would laugh a lot. I teased him, which he didn't mind. After a year, he declared his love for me over lunch in the manner of a medieval troubadour. I fell in love with him.

As the relationship wore on, 'he talked about divorce a lot but didn't do it', she says. 'Then one night he told Marina, who was devastated.' She adds:

But he lied about everything. He was jealous of other men who were successful, intelligent, good writers or attractive to women. He used to get very worked up about Simon Sebag Montefiore and Andrew Roberts, both of whom I knew and liked. After our relationship ended, I went to live in America and met someone else. He began ringing me all the time and trying to ruin the relationship. I got engaged and he rang up and told my fiancé that I was his girlfriend. He wrecked that relationship.

Miss Wyatt also tells a revealing anecdote about one occasion during their affair when she went to great lengths to make a seafood risotto for him. 'I knew he was a terrible timekeeper and I rang him telling him he had to be here by one o'clock as the risotto had to be eaten straight away,' she recalls.

He was late and I was furious with him. He cried when I scolded him. He cried more than any man I've known. Boris is like the unhappy clown. For him, it's all about winning, but it's not about the prize. That's because of his father. He did that to him. The reputation of the Johnsons is that they are this powerful dynasty, but I think they're just the poor man's Kennedys.

According to Miss Wyatt, the personalities of Carrie and Johnson are completely different.

Boris says yes to invitations, but actually he prefers the quiet life. Carrie parties at [clubs like] Loulou's and 5 Hertford Street, but he hates that. He is not a social animal. He was always worried about money. He was always talking about it. And he showed a surprising lack of sophistication. He once rejected a Pret A Manger sandwich as being too healthy. He prefers to eat sausages, cheap oven chips, Sunblest bread and sticky puddings. His idea of a gourmet supper is to eat at Pizza Express.

As the summer of 2018 turned to autumn and then winter, Johnson's morale is said to have slipped. 'He was increasingly isolated professionally and personally from all that he had known,' says one person who spent time with him then. 'It was a very difficult period in his life.' His burgeoning relationship with Carrie had not enhanced his political ambitions. Stuck in a cramped office in Westminster with only Lee Cain of his Foreign Office staff remaining, he buried himself in work, spending long hours trying to write a biography of William Shakespeare. He had originally signed a £500,000 contract with Hodder & Stoughton in 2015 to produce this book but had repeatedly postponed the project. Carrie is said to have continued to show an interest in reviving his political career at this time. 'She was still making suggestions about his media strategy,' remembers one figure.

> The trouble was, they were just very bad ideas. She once said he should give an interview to Rachel Sylvester of *The Times*. It had to be pointed out to her by Lee Cain, who was still working as his media spad, that a pro-Remain journalist like Rachel Sylvester was hardly likely to give the pro-Brexit Boris Johnson an easy time. Boris listened to Lee, and I think Carrie resented Lee for that. She disliked the fact that he had Boris's ear when it came to media strategy in a way that she did not.

One person whom she very much *did* like at that time, however, and with whom she spent an increasing amount of time, was the aforementioned Nimco Ali. They met in early 2018 and have been fast friends ever since. Miss Ali, who is five years older than Carrie, was born into a prosperous and influential family in Hargeisa, now the capital of Somaliland, and lived between Britain, Dubai and Somaliland from the age of four. When she was seven, she and her family were on holiday in Djibouti when she was subjected to a brutal operation on her genitalia which was carried out by a woman as part of a ritual that is common among young girls in certain parts of the world. Fleeing the Somali civil war of the 1980s, her father settled in Dubai, while she and her mother claimed asylum in Britain. They lived in Manchester before relocating to Cardiff, where, though Muslim, Miss Ali attended a Catholic school. She later read Law at the University of the West of England in Bristol and then worked as a civil servant before becoming an anti-female genital mutilation (FGM) campaigner. At the 2017 general election, she stood unsuccessfully for the Women's Equality Party. That year, she got to know Zac Goldsmith, who donated £1,000 to a fund she had started called Saving Mums' Lives in Somaliland. It is through her friendship with Goldsmith that she and Carrie are thought to have got to know each other.

In January 2018, Miss Ali gave an interview to the LBC radio presenter James O'Brien in which she discussed her own politics and anti-FGM activism, something which has led her to describe herself as a 'fanny defender'. She said that she feels at ease in Conservative Party circles but added: 'I'm more of a socialist … I don't really care what you do as your job as long as you pay your taxes. I'm very happy to say I'm a by-product of New Labour and I'm very comfortable within that setting.' In April 2018, Carrie posted a photograph of herself with Miss Ali on Instagram and wrote underneath it: 'One of the best things this year has been meeting [Nimco Ali]: A fanny-defending, feminist super babe. So excited for the work we'll do together & the turtles & camels we'll meet along the way.'

They seemed to become ever closer from that point. In July 2018, they both attended the Port Eliot Festival in Cornwall, where Miss

Ali was giving a talk about her activism. When Miss Ali wrote an opinion piece in the *Evening Standard* the following month, Carrie promoted it. And in October 2018, just a month after Carrie began her new job at Oceana – and while Boris Johnson attended the Conservative Party conference in Birmingham to build up his leadership credentials – Carrie and Miss Ali went to Somaliland together. While there, they are believed to have met the self-declared state's President, Muse Bihi Abdi, to discuss women's issues and pollution. Of this five-day trip, Carrie posted on Instagram a message which showed where her professional priorities now lay, to say nothing of her formidable range of contacts when it came to protecting wildlife. 'Last week [Nimco Ali] and I went to visit an incredible young woman who was trying to look after 13 cheetahs she had rescued after someone tried to smuggle them out to the UAE as pets and for their fur,' she wrote.

> Sadly she was not able to give them the care they really need and they were very likely going to die. So [Nimco] and I rang Zac Goldsmith MP and conservationist Damian Aspinall and asked them for help. Within 24 hours they'd sent out vets to Somaliland to treat the cheetahs and now they are working on getting them back to the wild where they belong. Couldn't be happier.

The *Mail on Sunday* was quick to speculate on the trip. It claimed that, unusually, Johnson had used a recent *Telegraph* column to pen what it called 'a paean of praise to the African elephant' and had urged the government to divert some of Britain's aid budget to conservation projects. His column, the paper believed, could be a 'disguised love letter' to Carrie. It further noted that Carrie's 'love of wildlife is said to extend to pet names. The 30-year-old is understood to affectionately call the former Foreign Secretary, 54, Bozzie the Bear, while he calls her Otter.'

In November 2018, Carrie took a trip to America. While there, she saw her friend Ben Mallett. By chance, her former boss John Whittingdale was also in the country and joined her and Mallett for lunch one day. She and Johnson then spent some time in New York, where, having signed up with an after-dinner speaking agency, he had secured a commission to give a speech to Golden Tree Asset Management in return for £95,000. They returned to London, where Carrie is known to have attended the *Spectator* awards ceremony later that month before flying back to Washington for work purposes. By now, Johnson, who had no permanent base in London following his marital separation, would sometimes stay at her flat in Camberwell. After Christmas, they flew to Greece together for a few days to stay at Stanley Johnson's villa. During this mini-break, a former Metropolitan Police inspector called Chris Wicks, who was also on holiday, spotted them sitting in a corner of the Aphrodite restaurant in Lafkos. They spoke briefly. Mr Wicks later told a newspaper that Johnson was 'very dishevelled, unshaven, [and was wearing] very tatty clothes'. Carrie was described as 'rather smartly dressed and quite sweet'.

Yet despite his unkempt appearance on holiday, it did not go unnoticed among fellow MPs and journalists in Westminster when he returned to London a few days later that Johnson had a sharper look about him. He had lost some weight and had his hair cut. With Theresa May's political fortunes flagging further, these were taken as outward signs that he had decided 2019 was the year that he had to make his move for the party leadership. Carrie still had her own professional commitments to Oceana, but it was soon equally clear to Johnson's political allies that she intended to be actively involved in the process which he hoped would take him to 10 Downing Street.

CHAPTER 8

PRINCESS NUT NUT

One Saturday afternoon in late January 2019, a few hundred demonstrators gathered in Cavendish Square in central London to protest against Japan's commercial whaling industry. The Japanese government had withdrawn from the International Whaling Commission and decided to allow whaling to resume for the first time in three decades. There were fears that this could result in many species of whales coming under threat. Carrie was among the protesters and held a placard bearing the logo of the Conservative Animal Welfare Foundation, of which she was still a patron, which stated simply 'End Whaling'. It had been agreed that a handful of people would give short speeches before everybody marched to the Embassy of Japan on Piccadilly. Among those who chose to speak were the animal rights activist Dominic Dyer; Will Travers of the Born Free Foundation; and Stanley Johnson, a longstanding environmentalist. Carrie also decided to address the crowd.

Boris Johnson was not present, but Carrie was supported by several close friends, including Alex Wickham. 'There can be no good reason to resume commercial whaling,' she said during her speech. 'We human beings are the custodians of this planet.' Her heartfelt comments were similar to ones made just a few weeks earlier by Johnson in his *Telegraph* column, in which he attacked the Japanese government for 'the brutal harpooning of beautiful, intelligent and endangered mammals'. He wrote: 'Just you try being harpooned. You see how you like it. It can take hours for whales to die – in extreme agony … To skewer such a creature, with a barbed and inaccurate lance, seems almost blasphemously cruel.' Her attendance at the rally was noted by the press, and some journalists were quick to suggest that it, coupled with Johnson's column, were carefully choreographed. It was as though they were using different platforms to promote shared causes. Carrie's job working for Oceana meant that she had professional reasons to be at the anti-whaling protest, of course, but what made the afternoon doubly significant in the eyes of some was Stanley Johnson's presence alongside her. The conclusion drawn was that Carrie's relationship with his eldest son had his blessing. This meant that he knew and liked her, in contrast to some other members of the Johnson family, notably Johnson's own children.

A few weeks later, in mid-February, a similar exercise took place. Shortly before going to New York for a mini-break to visit her friend Ben Mallett, Carrie accompanied Boris Johnson to Howletts Wild Animal Park in Kent. This somewhat unconventional zoo, which encourages close contact between animals and keepers, is run by a charity called the Aspinall Foundation, which was established by John Aspinall and is now run by his son Damian. Johnson and Carrie fed wildlife together, including gorillas, elephants and rhinos. They were also able to get very near some cheetahs. As an animal lover who was now earning a living through her interest in the natural world, this was a perfect excursion for Carrie. Johnson seems to have found the trip thought-provoking as well. The next day, the *Daily Telegraph* published an 1,100-word dispatch from Howletts written under his byline, titled 'What could be more British than saving Saba the cheetah from the ravages of man?' In the piece, he further cemented his commitment to protecting the natural world.

Whether this article was designed primarily to show that he had a caring side, as opposed to being obsessed solely with the issue of the day, Brexit, is a moot point. Four weeks earlier, however, he had made a wide-ranging speech that was highly critical of Theresa May, whose authority was diminishing daily because of the political complications of Brexit. This speech was regarded as his first proper pitch for the Tory leadership and he knew well enough that, in order to grasp that prize, projecting a hinterland could work in his favour. Speaking at the Staffordshire headquarters of the JCB tycoon Lord Bamford, Johnson discussed tax cuts and immigration limits as well as the ongoing Brexit saga. A small, unofficial campaign office had been set up by this point which Bamford and other businessmen were bankrolling. By March 2019, Lynton Crosby, the Australian election strategist, had been retained to advise Johnson. His leadership team was taking shape, therefore, but, despite the growing sense that he was in contention to become the next Prime Minister, he did allow himself some time off with his new girlfriend as spring blossomed.

In early March, Carrie flew to Abu Dhabi to attend a summit

on oceans. She returned to London and presented two prizes at the Green Heart Hero Awards, organised by the Climate Coalition and held in the Houses of Parliament. She also joined her friend Nimco Ali at an anti-female genital mutilation event at the Mayfair restaurant Sketch. Shortly afterwards, Johnson whisked her away to Positano in Italy for a few days to celebrate her 31st birthday. On Instagram, she posted a photograph of herself on a rather overcast Fornillo beach wearing a swimming costume to let her growing band of followers know that she was enjoying 'sunshine, swimming, Aperols and lots and lots of pasta'. One concerned friend pointed out: 'That beach looks... cold?' When the couple returned to London, there was more fun in store. Carrie's closest friends held a surprise birthday dinner for her at her favourite restaurant, Mamma Mia, in East Sheen, with Alex Wickham, Nimco Ali, Sophia True, Josh Grimstone and Henry Newman among the guests. Johnson also put in an appearance, arriving late by bicycle shortly before nine o'clock. Carrie, who subsequently described the occasion as 'one of the best nights ever', revealed: 'We even danced on the tables to ABBA.' As those gathered ate and drank, though, Johnson would have been forgiven for having other things on his mind. The screw was tightening on Theresa May. That night, she gave a televised speech at Downing Street to inform the nation that she knew the public had 'had enough' of Brexit and just wanted MPs to 'get on with it'. After the party, Carrie did not conceal her disdain for the Prime Minister. She later tweeted: 'Glad I didn't cancel my birthday dinner for that...'

All of this meant that the moment when a leadership contest would have to be held was drawing closer. Unable to win a parliamentary vote on Brexit, and with local Conservative Party associations increasingly uneasy, Mrs May told the 1922 Committee of backbench Tory MPs at a meeting on 27 March that she would stand down and allow a new Prime Minister to lead the UK in the next stage of Brexit negotiations if they voted to pass her deal. A few days later, in early April, the ranks of Johnson's leadership campaign team began to swell. It had already been decided that Lee Cain would be in charge of communications. Other non-MP team members were preparing for the race to begin. They included Lynton Crosby's colleague Mark Fullbrook; Alex Crowley; Rosie Bate-Williams; Will Walden; Ben Gascoigne; Shelley Williams-Walker; Alice Robinson; and Oliver Lewis.

Around this time, Johnson also asked a former Tory minister, James (now Lord) Wharton, to run the campaign as his chief of staff. Wharton asked for time to think about it and spent several days sounding out friends and allies. One Monday morning in mid-April, he went to see Johnson to tell him he would be happy to take on the job, only to be informed by a sheepish Johnson that the offer had been withdrawn. 'Boris told James that Carrie didn't trust him and she wanted a different person in that post,' says someone who worked on the campaign. Wharton was confused. He is said to have barely met Carrie by this point and he told Johnson that, apart from anything else, it was pretty widely known that he had been asked to fulfil this key campaign role.

Boris had to be told that if he sacked James, the papers would report that his campaign was in chaos before it had begun. So in order to accommodate Carrie's wishes, and to avoid humiliating himself, a line was agreed between James and Boris that James was setting up the campaign and would stay put until a full-time campaign chief had been found.

This person adds: 'I've never known why Carrie took against James. There may have been paranoia that James's friendship with Gavin Williamson, who was still Defence Secretary, could have compromised the campaign. After Gove knifed Boris in 2016, there was always paranoia.'

It was from this moment that everybody who was linked to Johnson's campaign realised the extent to which Carrie wanted to help her boyfriend achieve his long-held objective of becoming Prime Minister. 'It was a nightmare,' reports one source. 'She had no ideas, she wasn't prepared to roll her sleeves up and work hard, and yet she interfered all the time. This caused many problems and wasted a lot of very valuable time.' A second source adds:

> The problem was, she would want to control everything but she wouldn't work with anyone. There would be a team meeting, something would be decided and Boris would agree it. He would go home and tell Carrie everything that'd been decided and she would second-guess it all and then the phone would ring and it would be him saying, 'We've got to change this, we've got to do that, we're not going to do it like this any more.'

It has even been alleged that, on occasion, Carrie could be heard whispering prompts to Johnson while these calls were in progress.

'It was a very difficult environment to work in,' adds the second source. 'You'd think you'd got things agreed and they'd be second-guessed all the time when they were together alone in an environment to which none of us had access.'

Another source offers an example of how this unorthodox working arrangement backfired:

We were just getting things up and running. The campaign was a bit of a mess and had no structure. Nobody was doing Boris's social media. There was no social media strategy. So someone volunteered to do it. The campaign team got Boris's Twitter password and started putting out appropriate social media stuff. Then Boris came in the next day and said, 'I need my Twitter password.' He was told that candidates shouldn't do their own tweets, but eventually he got the password and, inevitably, there were mistakes.

One such error occurred on 2 May, when the local elections were held. Johnson is said to have gone home that evening. Soon after, a tweet appeared from his account which read: 'I just voted Conservative in the local elections. Make sure you do too! You've got two hours left to get out and vote!' It was immediately pointed out on Twitter to Johnson, who represents the west London constituency of Uxbridge and South Ruislip, that local elections were not taking place in London that day. His tweet was quickly deleted, but *The Guardian* got hold of the story. It later reported: 'After criticism, a source close to Johnson claimed he had voted near his second home in Thame in South Oxfordshire. He said he did not know why Johnson had deleted the tweet, and he could not explain why Johnson was registered to vote outside his Uxbridge constituency.'

The source explains: 'The official story was he'd voted in Thame. The fact that they deleted the tweet made it even worse as it looked like they were hiding something. Of course, it isn't sensible to advertise the fact that you don't live in your constituency.' The source goes on:

This is exactly what we didn't want to happen. There were lots of little things like that. When we were trying to persuade Tory MPs to support Boris, she [Carrie] used to compose tweets on things like saving elephants and FGM. These may be laudable issues, but they're not the issues you tweet about when you're trying to get MPs to vote for you in a leadership election. MPs are not the target audience for that sort of thing. So there were constant battles. There ended up being WhatsApp groups to agree what could be tweeted.

On 23 May, the EU elections were held and, as a result of Article 50 of the Treaty on European Union having been extended by six months to 31 October 2019, British voters participated in the ballot. The result was disastrous for Mrs May, with the Conservative Party finishing fifth overall. The next day, she announced that she would resign as Tory leader on 7 June and would then resign as Prime Minister as soon as a new leader had been chosen. Under an agreed timetable, nominations for the party leadership opened on 10 June. Ten candidates were in contention, including Johnson. The first ballot of MPs was held on 13 June, with subsequent ballots on 18, 19 and 20 June, by which date only two candidates would remain. After that, Conservative Party members would determine who would become their leader and, by extension, Prime Minister. The result would be announced on 23 July.

Johnson had kept a low profile over previous weeks, though by the time Mrs May announced her resignation timetable, his campaign headquarters had been established at the house of the Tory peer Greville Howard, in Lord North Street. Even before nominations opened, Johnson was the favourite to win. He had more critics on the Tory benches than any other leadership contender, but the party's poor standing in the opinion polls encouraged many Tory MPs to conclude that he represented their best chance of staying in power. This did not mean that the contest was plain sailing for him, however – or, indeed, for Carrie.

Johnson's campaign was officially launched at the Royal Academy of Engineering in Carlton House Terrace on the morning of 12 June. Perhaps surprisingly, he and Carrie had never been seen in public at an official event before then, despite the news of their relationship having broken nine months earlier. According to one member of the campaign team, Carrie seemed reluctant to be in her boyfriend's shadow.

On the day of his launch, we arranged that he would arrive by car. What does Carrie do? She arrives separately, gets out of her vehicle and walks quite a long way to the venue with her friend Nimco Ali by her side, so all the press became about her. She didn't tell the organisers she was coming, or if she did tell them, it was at the last minute. She could have gone in by a side door or something, but it had to be her big entrance. She claimed to hate being in the press, but she seemed to do all that she could to be centre stage. It was constant irritations like this that disrupted rather than derailed – but seriously diverted – attention from Boris, taking up a lot of people's time in a high-pressure situation.

Another source remembers a diary clash a few days later which proved awkward for Johnson. Again, Carrie is said to have been to blame. On 18 June, Johnson was due to attend a breakfast event for Conservative Party donors. It had been arranged by Ben Elliot, the nephew of Camilla Parker Bowles, who had carved out a reputation for himself as a first-rate fixer thanks to his impeccable contacts book. Yet according to this source, Carrie then insisted that Johnson should appear instead at a different breakfast event which was due to take place at the lobbying firm Brunswick at the same time. 'She organised it without telling anyone,' says the source.

Boris was told it was a bad idea. First, going to a lobbyists' breakfast in the middle of a leadership campaign is not a good look. Second, if he was going to do a lobbyists' breakfast, it should be very carefully thought through. It then became apparent that a friend of Carrie's called James Baker worked at Brunswick. She wanted Boris to do the Brunswick thing, and it didn't matter if it fitted with the campaign narrative or not. She'd just decided he was doing it without checking what was in his diary. So he ended up double-booked.

Matters came to a head. This person goes on:

> The night before, Boris rang James Wharton saying, 'I must do Brunswick.' James then rang around trying to sort it out. Carrie had apparently been whispering in Boris's ear, telling him what to say. In the end he did both breakfasts because he couldn't say no to her. He shouldn't have done this. It wasn't discussed as part of the process of the campaign and it upset some people on the campaign. This was the sort of thing that made everyone's life more difficult than it needed to be.

It has also been claimed that Carrie's apparent personal dislike of some members of the campaign team got the better of her. 'Behind the scenes, Boris's campaign was quite shambolic,' recalls a separate source. 'It hadn't attracted many people of high calibre. I think it was assumed it was well staffed, but that was not the case. Some good people did join halfway through, though. I remember Richard Holden came. So did Ellie Lyons. They became key components handling research and media.' Despite both team members becoming important to the operation, it has been alleged that Carrie did not approve of either of them.

As described in Chapter 5, Holden had worked with Carrie in the CCHQ press office several years previously. His life had been turned upside down when he was put on trial at Southwark Crown Court after being accused of groping a CCHQ aide at a Christmas party in 2016. Carrie was among those who gave evidence against him. The allegation was dismissed by a jury in May 2018 and Holden was allowed to leave court without a stain on his character.

Ellie Lyons was a bright and well-regarded CCHQ employee who had worked in the Conservative Research Department for two years before becoming a special adviser to Gavin Williamson when he was Chief Whip and then Defence Secretary, the latter post ending abruptly in early May 2019 when he was accused of leaking National Security Council information. Williamson and Lyons joined Johnson's campaign together.

Lyons did not know Carrie, but what happened next shocked some on the team. 'Boris started saying, "Let's get rid of Ellie,"' recalls one source.

> He said, 'Ellie is bad news.' He had to be told that Ellie had in fact made a brilliant contribution to the campaign and he was lucky to have her. It soon became apparent that this was another instruction from Carrie. There were similar noises about getting rid of Richard Holden. In order to shut down this nonsense, someone briefed the media that Richard and Ellie had joined the campaign so that it became impossible to get rid of them. Boris went nuts. But he was just being used by Carrie to do her dirty work.

The difficulties did not end there. It is also claimed that Carrie would make use of Johnson's telephone to try to direct and control events, though whether he was aware of this is unclear. 'She used to use his phone,' remembers one source.

> We'd spot the different ways things were written because the style would change. We'd learn to spot when it was her writing the message. So a text message would appear saying, for example,

that there was a particular MP whose support we didn't need or want. We realised Boris couldn't have written the message because the next day, Boris would contradict this.

What is more, Carrie also began to insist on a prominent role in the campaign for her friend Ben Mallett, who is close in age to her, and who drew attention to himself by carrying a briefcase. 'She finally brought in her friend Ben Mallett and said he had to be the campaign chief of staff,' remembers one source.

He's very nice, but there was no way he could run a campaign involving MPs. I think he'd recently returned from Yale, but everyone just looked at him and said: 'You're not just a child, you're a child with a briefcase. No one will take you seriously. You can't run this campaign.'

Another source adds:

Ben Mallett is nice, but he is not someone you would expect to run a serious political campaign. I think he had worked for Zac Goldsmith, which is how Carrie knew him. One day he walked in and announced he was now the campaign's chief of staff. We told him politely that this was rubbish. Boris said it was fine because he was too cowardly to confront Carrie about it. When some people threatened to quit if Ben Mallett really did become the chief of staff, Boris actually said, 'Can't you just *call* him the chief of staff?' He was told in no uncertain terms that this would not happen.

In the event, Mallett stayed on the campaign but in a lesser role. Attempts were also made by some on the team to sideline Carrie. These were not without comedy value.

> It got to the point where members of the team used to book taxis for her if there was a meeting that she was supposed to attend. The driver would be told to take the longest route possible to wherever the meeting was being held so that she would miss it. Sometimes this worked.

In light of all these allegations, perhaps it is no wonder that one junior member of Johnson's campaign team coined a nickname for Carrie during this period. 'She behaved like a princess, and she behaved in a way that was frankly nutty, so she became known as Princess Nut Nut', confirms one source. 'I can tell you categorically that Dominic Cummings was not the person who thought up this name.'

Things were about to turn significantly more serious, however. Shortly after midnight on Friday 21 June, police officers were called to Carrie's Camberwell flat after neighbours alerted them to what was described as a 'loud altercation involving screaming, slamming and banging'. *The Guardian* was tipped off about the story and ran it as an exclusive on its website that evening. It was revealed that a neighbour, later identified as Tom Penn, had recorded the disagreement between Carrie and Johnson from his own flat. He had apparently done so 'out of concern for the welfare of [Carrie]'. He had knocked on the door because he was worried about what was happening, but nobody had answered. *The Guardian* reported that

Penn had heard a woman screaming followed by 'slamming and banging'. At one point, Carrie could apparently be heard telling Johnson to 'get off me' and 'get out of my flat'. Although the police went into the flat, they left after being told by Carrie and Johnson that they were 'safe'.

Mr Penn's recording has never been heard in public, but a partial transcript of it was published by *The Guardian* as part of its coverage of the incident. According to the newspaper, Johnson can be heard in the recording refusing to leave the flat and telling Symonds to 'get off my fucking laptop' before there is a loud crashing noise. Carrie is heard saying that Johnson has ruined a sofa with red wine and telling him: 'You just don't care for anything because you're spoilt. You have no care for money or anything.' Mr Penn, then a playwright in his late twenties, told the paper:

> There was a smashing sound of what sounded like plates. There was a couple of very loud screams that I'm certain were Carrie and she was shouting to 'get out' a lot. She was saying 'get out of my flat' and he was saying no. And then there was silence after the screaming. My partner, who was in bed half asleep, had heard a loud bang and the house shook.

Remarkably, the first that anybody on Johnson's campaign team knew about this was when a *Guardian* reporter rang Lee Cain asking for a comment. None was forthcoming and Johnson is said never to have discussed the issue with anybody, shrouding its true cause in mystery. One possible clue as to why the eruption took place at all comes from Petronella Wyatt. It is known that she once sent Johnson a text message in which she wrote: 'She [Carrie] needs her teeth fixed.' Since it was revealed in April 2021 that Johnson was still using the same publicly available mobile phone number he had had for at least fifteen years and he is not thought to have been careful about changing the password on his mobile device, it is possible Carrie became aware of this comment, triggering the row. Whatever the truth, the situation had to be put right quickly.

The incident was picked up by other newspapers for their Saturday editions on 22 June. That afternoon, Johnson, whose only rival for the leadership by then was Jeremy Hunt, was due to give an interview in front of thousands of Conservative Party members in Birmingham to the journalist Iain Dale, who interviewed every candidate during the leadership contest. 'You know as well as I do that there is only one subject on everybody's lips today,' Dale said. 'And they want to know why the police were called to your house in the early hours of Friday morning.' A ripple of laughter was heard from those gathered as Johnson smiled and shifted in his seat. He remained composed. After thanking those who had come to the hustings, he said: 'Iain, listen, I think what people have come here today [to hear], seductive interviewer though you are ... I don't think they want to hear about that kind of thing.' There was a burst of applause. 'I think what they want to hear is what my plans are for the country and for our party.' Dale tried again, pointing out that it was 'everybody's business' if somebody on the brink of becoming Prime Minister had received a visit from the police. He made several more attempts. Johnson stonewalled every one.

All of the Sunday newspapers fixated on the affair, but the

coverage in the *Mail on Sunday* was noticeably insightful. It informed readers of the gravity of the situation for Johnson by publishing the results of two surveys, one taken before the row and the other taken afterwards. Jeremy Hunt had dissolved Johnson's eight-point lead and turned it into a three-point deficit. Hunt was now the favourite to succeed Theresa May, though this would not last. The paper also had information about Tom Penn and his girlfriend, Eve Leigh, Carrie's neighbours who had rung the police and then given a recording of the row to *The Guardian*. Mr Penn confirmed that he was opposed to Brexit while Ms Leigh had reportedly in the past 'made offensive gestures towards Mr Johnson when they met on the steps of the building'. The article went on: 'This newspaper understands that when encountering Ms Leigh last month, Mr Johnson said hello but she replied by sticking two fingers up at him. Friends of Mr Johnson say he was astonished at how aggressive the gesture had been.' The paper further described 'increasing hostility' towards Johnson in the neighbourhood. 'His car has been covered with posters denouncing him, while the couple's home has been plastered with stickers reading F*** Boris. The pair have received at least 14 items of hate mail through the letterbox in the past week.' It did not go unnoticed that Harry Cole, Carrie's former boyfriend who was by then the deputy political editor of the *Mail on Sunday*, had a byline on the story.

The *Sunday Times* also put one of its senior reporters onto the story. He was Andrew Gilligan, a longstanding ally of Johnson. He had more insights which were useful in getting across points Johnson no doubt felt were important, including a detailed description of the interior of the building where the flat was situated. 'Friends of Symonds said her anger over the incident was directed at Penn and Leigh rather than Johnson,' the paper reported.

> They said she believed her neighbours' decision to record the incident and give the tape to a left-wing newspaper was a 'dirty tricks story' and she felt 'very unlucky' to have Penn and Leigh living across the landing from her. The friends said Symonds accused Leigh and Penn of 'eavesdropping' on the couple during the event.

Then one friend gave the following quote: 'Carrie feels trapped in the flat and does not feel safe after this.' The paper added that neither Carrie nor Johnson had heard Leigh or Penn knocking on their door as they rowed. Both apparently knew Carrie's mobile number but had not called it.

On Monday 24 June, some newspapers published a photograph of Carrie and Johnson sitting around a table in a rural setting, apparently in Sussex, smiling and talking. It was billed as being the first time they had been pictured together since the row. Few believed the scene had not been staged in order to gloss over the problem. Some in the media went further, suggesting that it was in fact an old photograph which had been taken before the row had happened. On Tuesday 25 June, Johnson gave an interview to the LBC radio presenter Nick Ferrari. Again, he was defensive. He refused to tell Ferrari when the photo had been taken, even after it was pointed out to him that his hair in the picture seemed to be longer than it had been the day before it was taken, Saturday, and longer than it was at that moment in time. Again, he stonewalled.

The dent that this domestic dispute put into Johnson's campaign is said to have prompted some of his closest advisers, including Lynton Crosby, to speak to him directly. 'Boris was told to get rid of Carrie,' says one source. Carrie is said to have found out about this. 'I believe Lynton was frozen out.' A friendlier, if more bizarre, interview that day was conducted by Carrie's friend Ross Kempsell on TalkRadio. In it, Johnson revealed that he relaxes by making models of buses, an unexpected hobby that, usefully, generated much comment.

For Carrie, however, worse, arguably, was to come. In early July, she spent a bit of time away from the campaign. On Saturday 6 July, she attended a Celine Dion concert in Hyde Park. She also posted a picture on Instagram of herself with a friend, the aforementioned James Baker of Brunswick, supporting the Gay Pride parade, which took place that day. Any calm was soon shattered. On the evening of 9 July, Johnson was in Manchester for a live TV debate against Jeremy Hunt which was chaired by the journalist Julie Etchingham and shown on ITV. Carrie was in London, where the *Daily Mail* journalist Simon Walters had been working on the story outlined in Chapter 6, which revealed that she had been forced to resign as CCHQ's director of communications in 2018 because of her expenses claims and her performance at work. Early editions of the *Mail* splashed on this previously unknown element of her past that night. A source says: 'Carrie went ballistic. She rang Boris in Manchester and demanded that he return to London, which he did.' A hunt for the source of the story began. Several high-profile people were accused, each of whom strongly rejected the claim that they had been involved. 'She demanded that Boris fire whoever was responsible for the leak.' This never happened. The matter was eventually left to one side.

Looking back on the exhausting leadership campaign, one figure who has given careful thought to Carrie's behaviour during it reflects ruefully on their impression of the role she played. 'She could be utterly charming, but she was always working behind the scenes,' says this person.

She's a spoilt kid, a bit of a princess who wants it all her own way. Just because she can't have her own way doesn't mean the person stopping her hates her, but she seems to see it in black and white terms: you are my enemy and I will destroy you. Even if her way is something ridiculous that shouldn't happen, if you're the one who tells her that it can't happen, she turns on you. There was an entitlement and an insecurity about her, and a lack of intellectual depth. She's got a view of how she should be seen in the media. She thinks people should love her and think highly of her and that she's a loving, wonderful person, and she's not. I would say Boris is trapped in an emotionally disruptive relationship. I think he's definitely scared of her and I think she dominates him. There were moments where he knew he was insisting on things that were not good for his campaign. And in private moments he would say words to the effect of: 'Don't do anything that's going to make her torture me when I get home. You've just got to help me. My life at home's miserable. You've got to find a way to make this bearable for me.' He'd speak with exasperation in his eyes. There's something not right about her. There's something more to it than being just about her ego. It's about getting her own way, getting even with people who've slighted her. One of her least attractive traits is wanting to settle scores with those who she feels have slighted her, even when they might not have. She's callous as to the impact she has on people's lives. Sometimes you get on with people, sometimes you don't, but you don't have to take issue with everybody who disagrees with you.

Even after suffering such serious knocks during the campaign, Johnson was crowned party leader shortly after noon on 23 July. The announcement was made at the Queen Elizabeth II conference centre in central London. About 160,000 Conservative Party members were entitled to vote in the ballot. The final result confirmed that Johnson had won a convincing victory, securing 92,153 votes to Jeremy Hunt's 46,656. His father, Stanley, and siblings Jo – who was still an MP himself – and Rachel, looked on. Carrie was also in evidence. The next day, 24 July, Johnson was invited by the Queen to form a government. As with so much about Johnson, he entered Downing Street differently to any of his recent predecessors. Whereas all but one previous Prime Minister in living memory had arrived at the centre of Britain's power – and their new home – with a spouse, Johnson took up the mantle as a man who was finalising his divorce from his second wife. As he delivered his first speech from Downing Street, Carrie was among the group of aides and supporters who stood alongside him listening. No member of his family was there to celebrate with him as he embraced his dream.

In that week's *Spectator*, the magazine Johnson used to edit, Paul Dacre, the former editor of the *Daily Mail*, wrote:

So the party of family values has chosen as leader a man of whom to say he has the morals of an alley cat would be to libel the feline species. Thus the Tories, with two women PMs to their credit, have achieved another historic first: scuppering the belief – argued by the *Daily Mail* in my 26 years as editor – that politicians with scandalous private lives cannot hold high office. I make no comment on this, or about the 31-year-old minx who is the current Boris Johnson bedwarmer, but ask you instead to spare a thought for Petronella's abortion, Helen's love child, Marina's humiliation and her four children's agony … As for the Minx, mark my words: there will be tears before midnight.

CHAPTER 9

'WATCH CARRIE GO TO WORK ON HIM NOW'

The role of the prime ministerial consort in Britain is far from straightforward and whoever occupies this position must accept some hard realities. As one former Downing Street resident, Cherie Blair, wrote in her book *The Goldfish Bowl*, which she co-authored with Cate Haste: 'There is no job description for the Prime Minister's spouse because there is no job.' Mrs Blair, who has met the husband or wife of every Prime Minister to hold office between 1955 and 2010, went on to explain that 'each [spouse] has defined their own role according to their time, personality and the circumstances they encountered'. She added that the common thread shared by every consort she has met was their knowledge that 'their main role was to be a support and comfort to the Prime Minister'. Through a series of interviews with seven prime ministerial spouses, *The Goldfish Bowl* offers fascinating insights into what life behind the famous black door has been like for them. It shows that being married to a Prime Minister and living in Downing Street is not as glamorous or as easy as some people might assume, requiring superhuman levels of tact and discretion. As Britain's first male prime ministerial consort, Denis (later Sir Denis) Thatcher, who occupied the role for eleven years, once remarked: 'The longer you keep your mouth shut, the safer you are.'

Carrie entered this unique environment in July 2019 facing certain complications. For one, she was to live in Downing Street as the first unmarried partner of a Prime Minister in British history. This in itself generated a considerable amount of comment. What made the circumstances under which she set up home there somewhat stranger was that, thanks to her professional background and relationships, she was also the first partner of any Prime Minister to be part of what is known as 'the Westminster bubble' – that is to say, the insular world of Lobby journalists, politicians and special advisers who live and breathe the goings-on in Westminster and Whitehall. On the one hand, she stuck out because of her status as the Prime Minister's girlfriend; on the other, she was already part of the Westminster club, which can be seen as rather cosy.

Added to this, it is fair to say that until July 2019, no previous Prime Minister's partner had had any idea when they embarked on a relationship with their future husband or wife that they would one day find themselves living in Downing Street, with the possible exception of Clarissa Eden, whose husband Sir Anthony Eden was considered the heir apparent to her uncle, Sir Winston Churchill, long before he took office in 1955. Carrie's and Johnson's relationship resembled the Edens' to an extent when they arrived in Downing Street. Like Johnson, Sir Anthony Eden, a divorcee, was a former Foreign Secretary who was twenty-three years older than his wife, who was in her early thirties. But of course, the Edens had the protective layer of a marriage to offer them some security, even if they were still the subject of gossip and backbiting. Johnson and Carrie had no such comfort.

Furthermore, there is no question that when they began seeing one another in 2018, Johnson not only *wanted* to be Prime Minister; he also had a realistic prospect of *becoming* Prime Minister. That is not to suggest that Carrie took up with him for this reason. It is simply to make the point that for most of the eighteen or so months that they had been together before they moved into Downing Street, the idea of his soon leading the country had been discussed in serious terms pretty consistently, whether by them, their colleagues or the press, thereby placing this high-profile aim at the centre of their relationship.

And yet despite this, the speed with which events moved in the spring and summer of 2019 meant that the public to some degree had Carrie to accept with little warning. While it is true that John and Norma Major moved into Downing Street very abruptly in November 1990 when Norma was less well known than Carrie in July 2019, the Majors did have the advantage of convention on their side in the form of a twenty-year marriage. Most people who had even heard of Carrie in July 2019 probably only knew that she had been named as the young lady accused of being at the centre of Johnson's divorce from his second wife, Marina; or that there had been a domestic dispute at her flat the previous month to which the police had been called. Who can say what extra pressure these intricacies and complexities placed on Carrie and, indeed, on Boris Johnson when they reached Downing Street?

Aside from any judgements about their personal lives, however,

Boris Johnson had more pressing matters with which to wrestle, namely Brexit. Three years had passed since the referendum result which saw the public vote in favour of Britain leaving the European Union, yet that departure had still not been negotiated let alone achieved. This seemingly intractable problem had destroyed Theresa May's premiership and left many members of every political party in the House of Commons bearing battle scars. Johnson had promised the country that he would end the deadlock, but he knew that further skirmishes lay ahead.

Like all new Prime Ministers, he spent his first few days in post appointing his Cabinet and choosing the team who would work around him in Downing Street. His decision to ask his younger brother, Jo – who had been staunchly opposed to Brexit – to be an Education Minister and to attend Cabinet was not anticipated and pointed to a desire for political unity. Likewise making another Remainer, Sajid Javid, Chancellor of the Exchequer. Two non-MP appointments that Johnson wanted to make on entering Downing Street proved trickier to arrange, however. There was surprise from close aides at his insistence that Alex Wickham should be the No. 10 press secretary and that Ross Kempsell should be installed as head of broadcast. Both were journalists who were close friends of Carrie; both were under the age of thirty and neither had ever worked in a political environment before. Lee Cain, who had already been promised the role of director of communications, made his displeasure known to Johnson. 'Lee told Boris he would leave if either Wickham or Kempsell were given these jobs,' says a source who worked in Downing Street at the time. 'After the interference Carrie had been responsible for during the leadership campaign,

Lee knew that hiring them would be a huge mistake. Boris told Lee that Carrie would be cross with him if her friends were not given jobs, but Lee stood firm.' Neither Wickham nor Kempsell was given a job at that point.

One appointment that Cain and Johnson did agree on was that of Dominic Cummings as his chief adviser. During negotiations, Cummings made clear to Johnson that he would accept the job but he would need to have it in writing that he would be granted the power to employ and dismiss staff as he saw fit. Johnson agreed to this. Indeed, in many ways the level of authority that Cummings requested chimed with the overall model of governing that he, Cain and Johnson wished to follow. They were all familiar with Chris Whipple's 2017 book *The Gatekeepers: How the White House Chiefs of Staff Define Every Presidency* and had concluded that Johnson's premiership would work best if it were close in style and management to Ronald Reagan's presidency, with Johnson adopting the role of the optimistic leader and Cummings and Cain overseeing the engine room and making staffing decisions. It seems that this idea had Carrie's approval as well. 'I can remember Carrie telling me it was a brilliant appointment, that he [Cummings] was a genius,' recalls John Whittingdale.

During those early months of Johnson's first administration, Carrie was busy with matters besides politics, notably concerning finances. During the week that he became Prime Minister, she and Johnson completed a deal to buy a house together in Camberwell. The four-bedroom terraced property, purchased with a mortgage, cost £1.2 million. As both of them owned other properties at the time, the new house was classed as a second property for tax purposes, incurring stamp duty of £99,750. It was also felt worthwhile to inform the media that Carrie would be the first female prime ministerial partner since Norma Major not to have a taxpayer-funded office with a full-time member of staff to organise her diary, host charity events and handle media enquiries. The *Daily Mail* further reported that the couple 'would not be using money from the public coffers to buy a bed or any furniture'. These cost-cutting measures appeared to go down well with the press.

In mid-August, Carrie then undertook her first public speaking engagement, by which point some media outlets had begun to dub her the 'First Girlfriend'. Her appearance at the Bird Fair birdwatching conference in Rutland had in fact been agreed three months beforehand, before anybody could be certain that she would be living in Downing Street. At the event, she gave a short speech and then took part in a *Question Time*-style panel with Dominic Dyer, the head of the Badger Trust; and the BBC presenters Chris Packham and Deborah Meaden. Shortly beforehand, she condemned British hunters who travel to Iceland to shoot puffins and bring their carcasses home as trophies, tweeting: 'Just can't understand why anyone would want to shoot them. Mad.'

Many people would agree that shooting a vulnerable species for fun is indeed 'mad'. Yet what nobody who read that message knew was that Carrie was shortly to be linked to a similarly ruthless act which ended the career of a promising young Downing Street aide. The previous chapter described how Carrie asked Johnson during his leadership campaign to remove from his team a political adviser called Ellie Lyons. The plan backfired when another member of the team informed the media that Miss Lyons, a Cambridge graduate, was working on the campaign, thus making it impossible to dispense with her services. Having been impressed with Miss Lyons's performance on the campaign, Johnson had asked her to join his Downing Street operation as head of the political unit. After about a month, however, she was dismissed. A source says:

> I think Carrie had spent the weekend at Chequers. One Monday morning, Dominic Cummings told Ellie that she was being let go. It was very abrupt, totally unexpected, and there had been no problem that Ellie was aware of. Nobody knew why it happened, but it had a big impact on Ellie's life. She hardly knew Carrie, but it didn't take long for it to become clear that Carrie didn't want her there.

Another source adds:

> We learned pretty quickly there was a culture of fear around touching anything that Carrie didn't like. There was a nervousness. I think the people who are close to her and align with her get great benefits. Those who idolise her might get a fantastic job out of it. If she doesn't like you, there can be big consequences.

A third source says: 'She doesn't like people who are more intelligent or attractive than her around her. Ellie's problem was that she is both attractive and intelligent.'

Johnson might have had other matters on his mind that month. On 11 August, the *Sunday Times* revealed that his estranged wife Marina had received treatment for cervical cancer earlier that year.

She had written a piece for the newspaper about the experience and urged other women to undergo smear tests. Despite having regular screenings herself in the past, she admitted that she had left it late. 'Something else always seemed more important,' she wrote. 'If you are basically healthy, active and energetic, it is easy to think you are immortal, but none of us is.' As she recovered in hospital, she admitted her 'spirits dipped' and her despair even led her to try to walk out of the hospital. She was found and brought back to the ward where her family were waiting. 'After hugging, we all relaxed and soon they offered helpful ways to view the situation.' Ms Wheeler underwent three operations at University College Hospital in London. She made clear how crucial the support of her family, including her children, had been. Yet her sister, Shirin, was singled out for praise. 'Shirin has been my saviour,' she wrote. 'She was with me all the time and kept friends and family in the loop. She was endlessly attentive and took the unsavoury stuff in her stride.' Ms Wheeler wrote that the entire episode had made her appreciate 'the incalculable value of holding close those who you love and trust'. Her husband's name was not mentioned in the article.

It is said often that Johnson has few, if any, friends, and that behind the mask is something of a loner. Yet former colleagues of his believe that, throughout their marriage, Marina was his mainstay. One person who knows Johnson well, having worked with him when he was the Mayor of London, says:

Marina was a very important influence on Boris. She was always punctual, she'd remember people's birthdays and there was a basic human decency to her. She cared. She instilled order. And she is very intelligent. I don't remember her expressing strong political views. I don't think she was ideologically aligned with Boris, but she was like a chief executive, managing Boris and keeping him on the straight and narrow path. When the marriage ended, he lost his domestic support, the steadying influence, and he traded that in for a demanding girlfriend and strong disapproval from his children. Do not underestimate how destabilising all of that can be. At the start of his time in Downing Street, he had to deal with the Brexit crisis, having no parliamentary majority and none of his children talking to him. It is, for me, a huge part, and an under-reported part, of the chaos of his premiership. I think everyone has treated it lightly, but if we ignore it, we fail to understand what has really been going on. Boris has always needed someone to make sure he has money in his pocket and a clean suit and shirt. There is a big management role in keeping him on a straight line. He went from having a base run by someone who knows him well – Marina – to an arrangement where home wasn't properly organised and the person in that home, Carrie, is demanding rather than supplying. I think it's the biggest explanation of the dysfunctionality inside No. 10 and I cannot believe he wasn't aware of it at this time. Marina was his wife, but she was also, in some respects, a mother figure to him.

On 2 September, a new resident moved into Downing Street in the form of a puppy called Dilyn. Photographs of Carrie holding the Jack Russell in the Downing Street garden were circulated and a quote from Johnson's official spokesperson was provided, praising the Friends of Animals Wales charity which rescued the dog after it discovered it was going to be dumped by a puppy dealer because it had been born with a crooked jaw. The Prime Minister's spokesperson was unable to confirm whether the puppy, which was a few months old, had been housetrained. In a statement, Friends of Animals Wales said:

> We knew that Carrie Symonds has always been a huge animal welfare advocate and we are absolutely overjoyed that this gorgeous pup will be living his best life with Carrie and the Prime Minister at their Downing Street home. To think our little 'wonky' pup started his life in a Welsh puppy farm and was destined for an uncertain existence at the hands of a puppy dealer, but is now going to be with people who absolutely adore him is a dream come true. This little man will want for nothing in his life, what could be better than that?

Carrie plastered her Instagram account with photos of the dog for the next few days while Johnson focused on matters of state.

On 5 September, his brother Jo announced his resignation from the Cabinet. His departure is said to have rattled Johnson, who was visiting a police training academy in West Yorkshire when the news became public. Jo Johnson posted on Twitter a brief explanation of why he had quit. 'In recent weeks I've been torn between family loyalty and the national interest,' he wrote. 'It's an unresolvable tension & time for others to take on my roles as MP & Minister. #overandout'. *The Sun* reckoned that there were both personal and political reasons for the surprise move. Although Brexit was a factor, the paper mentioned that his wife, a *Guardian* journalist called Amelia Gentleman, had been involved in his decision. A source close to Ms Gentleman was quoted saying: 'She hated to see her beloved sister-in-law being put through the mill by Boris. While Marina was recovering from two operations for cervical cancer, Boris was off gallivanting with Carrie Symonds. It didn't sit well with her and she gave Jo a very hard time over it.'

The following day, Johnson and Carrie flew to Aberdeenshire, where they were to stay at Balmoral, the Queen's estate. Every year, the Queen spends the summer there. Usually, she is joined by other members of the royal family and hosts the Prime Minister for three days in September. Then ninety-three years old, this was the first time in the monarch's long reign that she had received a visit from a Prime Minister who was not married to his partner. One source who knows the Queen has confirmed that she felt awkward about the arrangement:

Bearing in mind the Queen's age and the generation that she belongs to, I know that she was unhappy about Boris Johnson staying at Balmoral with Carrie in 2019. She did not think it was appropriate and I think it would have been easier for her if Boris had gone there alone.

In the event, the visiting couple stayed for only one night, not three as is customary. The reason for this was that Johnson was seeking to call a general election at the time but was being thwarted by the Labour Party and the SNP, both of which promised to block any poll until an extension to the Brexit deadline had been secured. He had to be in London to monitor events.

A couple of days later, on 9 September, *The Times* revealed that the government had intervened to stop thousands of badgers being culled in Derbyshire by refusing to grant licences to farmers who wanted to carry out this exercise to stop the spread of tuberculosis. The paper then disclosed that Carrie had met Dominic Dyer, the chief executive of the Badger Trust, in Downing Street two days before they appeared together at the Bird Fair festival in mid-August. Dyer subsequently sent Carrie details of the case for refusing a culling licence in Derbyshire, together with a copy of a letter to Boris Johnson, dated 3 September, in which Dyer wrote that a cull in Derbyshire risked killing badgers that had been vaccinated at public expense. '[Carrie] told friends she was delighted by the decision to protect Derbyshire's badgers but is understood to be denying any involvement in it,' the paper stated. 'She is a longstanding opponent of badger culling.' Dyer told *The Times*:

> I have every reason to believe this decision was taken as a direct intervention by the prime minister, who recognised the absurdity of spending over half a million pounds to police a cull in the county, to enable cull contractors to shoot badgers that have been vaccinated against TB, under a public-funded programme.

The story did nothing to quell mounting speculation of Carrie's influence on her then boyfriend.

There was further discomfort for him a couple of weeks later when, on 22 September, the *Sunday Times* revealed for the first time his links to Jennifer Arcuri, the American businesswoman he had met and become involved with in 2012. The newspaper claimed that he had failed to declare a series of potential conflicts of interest over his friendship with Arcuri when he was Mayor of London. It stated that Arcuri was given £126,000 of public money and what it called 'privileged access' to three overseas trade missions led by Johnson. Although the report was careful to avoid stating as fact that they were anything other than friends, it did state that 'Johnson was a regular visitor to Arcuri's top-floor flat in Shoreditch, east London'. Carrie's reaction to this news is unknown. She was preparing to fly to New York with her friend Nimco Ali to attend the fourth annual Goalkeepers Global Goals Awards, which acknowledges outstanding work around the world that is directly linked to the United Nations Sustainable Development Goals.

Yet when she returned, the *Sunday Times* made a further, separate allegation against Johnson in its next edition. This time, an article written by journalist Charlotte Edwardes claimed that several years earlier, when Johnson edited *The Spectator*, he had touched her leg inappropriately while having lunch. 'Under the table, I feel Johnson's hand on my thigh,' she wrote.

> He gives it a squeeze. His hand is high up my leg and he has enough inner flesh beneath his fingers to make me sit suddenly upright. My mother always said: 'Wear a badge to the cinema with which to stab the wandering hands.' But this is work, so I am silent.

Edwardes then claimed that afterwards she confided in the young woman sitting on Johnson's other side, who said, 'Oh God, he did exactly the same to me.' Even though it was hard for anybody to prove what had happened more than a decade earlier, it was hardly dignified for a sitting Prime Minister to be accused of such behaviour.

That weekend marked the start of the annual Conservative Party conference, which was held in Manchester. Johnson and Carrie arrived together, arm in arm, leaving little room for doubt that their relationship was serious. One source says that, by this point, Johnson's former adviser, Lynton Crosby, warned him that if he intended to stay with Carrie, he should have a vasectomy. 'I recall Lynton telling me that he'd advised Boris that if he was going to stay with Carrie, he should have the snip,' says a source. As the conference began, Tom Newton Dunn, the political editor of *The Sun*, published a story claiming that some of Johnson's longstanding allies had accused him of 'shutting them out' and only listening to two people: Dominic Cummings and Carrie. The paper claimed that Johnson had had 'bitter rows' with his former advisers Lynton Crosby and Will Walden. Walden, it was revealed, had refused to take up a role in No. 10 after feeling 'marginalised' and had gone to work in the private sector – an idea that others have since confirmed. One unnamed senior minister was quoted in the story saying that, by this point, Johnson distrusted anyone who was critical of Carrie. 'He is paranoid about her. His regular refrain is "they're just saying that because they want to get Carrie". It's really not helpful as he's shut everyone else out now.' Another ally of Johnson is said to have told the paper: 'Carrie fucked with his mind. She has him completely mesmerised.'

After the conference had ended, Carrie's next stop was Amsterdam, which she visited for a meeting in conjunction with her role as an adviser to Oceana. On her return, she went with her former boyfriend Harry Cole and Nimco Ali to Mamma Mia The Party, a live show and four-course meal in London set to the music of her favourite band, ABBA. By this time, Johnson's government was tabling a series of parliamentary motions calling for a general election. Finally, it was agreed that the snap poll would take place on 12 December 2019. Carrie was an enthusiastic campaigner, criss-crossing the country over the course of several weeks in support of different Tory candidates, all seeking election under the promise that the Conservatives were going to 'Get Brexit Done'.

On the night of the vote, an exit poll released by the BBC just after ten o'clock predicted that the Tories had won the election with a majority of eighty-six seats. This turned out to be a slight exaggeration – the true majority being eighty seats – but it was the confirmation Johnson and Carrie needed that they would not be moving out of No. 10 that weekend. Indeed, on the strength of the result, it appeared very much as though they might be there for some time. Everybody in Downing Street was in celebratory mood over the next few days, unable to grasp the scale of the victory that had been achieved under Johnson. There had been nothing like it since the days of Margaret Thatcher in the 1980s. One person saw things differently, however. Dominic Cummings was by then only too aware of Carrie's needs and wants taking up an increasing amount of Johnson's time, to say nothing of her willingness to meddle as she saw fit in staffing matters and, perhaps, policy matters as well. His

view was that the large majority the Tories had secured was certain to mean that she would seek to entrench her position. When
one close colleague sought a congratulatory chat with Cummings,
his response was short and to the point. 'This is a disaster,' he said.
'Watch Carrie go to work on him now. I give it six months before
we're out of a job.'

CHAPTER 10

HATCHES, MATCHES, DISPATCHES

On the morning of Friday 13 December 2019, the ITV programme *Good Morning Britain* gathered together a group of panellists which included Boris Johnson's sister, Rachel, and father, Stanley, to discuss the Conservatives' landslide victory the night before. During their conversation, the presenter, Piers Morgan, asked Rachel Johnson: 'Can we talk about one other person in all of this who has been a bit of a star: Carrie.' Appearing flummoxed, Rachel replied: 'I haven't met Carrie.' Morgan retorted: 'You've never *met* her?' Shrugging her shoulders, Rachel was tongue-tied momentarily but added: 'Not yet. Well, it's not something I came to talk about [today].' 'Blimey,' said Morgan. He then turned to Stanley Johnson and asked him if he'd met Carrie. Stanley replied: 'I share an interest in environmental matters, I share an interest in animal welfare matters. I've had the privilege of talking about Japanese whaling after Carrie or before Carrie. I've talked about elephants, I have talked about rats.' In order to clarify his question, Morgan interrupted to ask: 'You haven't met her, Stanley?' To which Stanley said: 'Of course I've met her.' The damage, however, was done. No sooner had this apparent awkwardness been exposed on live television than people voiced their suspicions. Why had the Prime Minister's sister, Rachel – the sibling to whom he is closest – not yet met Carrie? After all, almost two years had passed since the couple's 2018 Valentine's Day assignation at Rules restaurant.

Carrie and Johnson spent Christmas Day of 2019 at Downing Street rather than at Chequers, as is customary for Prime Ministers, though by then Carrie had made good use of this official retreat in rural Buckinghamshire, appreciating the privacy it allows. On Boxing Day, the couple flew to the private Caribbean island of Mustique, where they were staying rent-free in a villa which came with a butler, chef and housekeeper and which would normally have cost them £15,000 for a week. The identity of the generous benefactor who gave them the keys to this idyllic property was not revealed. Newspapers were soon told, however, that the thrifty couple had bought themselves £1,300 Economy-class tickets for their British Airways flight to St Lucia, where they changed planes, instead of using an RAF plane at a public cost of £100,000. A few days after Christmas, the *Mail on Sunday* added to the theme of prudence by disclosing that Carrie had given Johnson a second-hand Yamaha motorbike for Christmas which had cost about £1,000. The byline of her former boyfriend, Harry Cole, was on this light-hearted story.

The peace of their winter holiday was broken on 3 January 2020 when reports surfaced of American forces having assassinated General Qasem Soleimani, Iran's most senior military commander. British government sources explained to the media that the UK had received no advance notice of the attack at Baghdad International Airport, which was carried out by a drone, and had been briefed only once the mission was underway. Johnson is said to have been kept informed of the incident while he was in the Caribbean, but when some MPs advanced the idea that Parliament should be recalled to discuss this new Middle East crisis, they were dismissed. Johnson and Carrie returned to London from their holiday two days later, but some commentators feared that Johnson might have failed his first big test as the newly elected Prime Minister and, worse still, that he might have put his personal pleasure, and that of his girlfriend, ahead of his duty. One person who worked closely with Johnson at the time is not surprised by the laidback approach he took on that occasion.

There was a feeling in Downing Street that after the election victory, Boris thought his eighty-seat majority would allow him to coast. Dominic Cummings was eager to hit the ground running. He was incredibly serious about carrying out a series of major reforms in Whitehall and elsewhere. But in meetings Boris behaved like a clown. He would tell jokes. People would laugh. Dominic really disapproved of this. He ended up telling people not to laugh at Boris's jokes because laughing only encouraged him.

The date of 31 January 2020 had been in the diary of many Brexiteers for weeks, as it marked the point, after months of bitter wrangling, that Britain would formally leave the European Union. The Brexit Party leader, Nigel Farage, had organised a gathering of tens of thousands in Parliament Square to mark the historic occasion, but Johnson refused to attend it. Instead, he hosted a low-key party in Downing Street to which a group of ministers and advisers were invited. Dominic Cummings and Lee Cain were also present. They drank English sparkling wine and ate British foods including roast beef and Yorkshire pudding, savoury shortbread topped with Shropshire blue cheese, and a ploughman's of cheddar and pickle. The evening intentionally lacked any sense of triumphalism and soon after the clock struck eleven, and Britain's separation from the bloc was official, guests drifted off. Upstairs in the spacious flat above 11 Downing Street, where Johnson and Carrie had been living since the summer, another party was just getting going. Attended mainly by friends of Carrie, it was an altogether livelier affair. Dancing was encouraged and her favourite band, ABBA, played on the stereo. One report of the soiree presents Johnson in a rather unflattering light. 'Boris was pretty much ordered to dance,' says one source. 'Everyone was whooping and cheering as he did so. For a few seconds it was as though he was one of those dancing Russian bears, performing under instruction. There was something rather sad about it.' The sense that Carrie seemed to want to exercise control over Johnson, and to be involved in decisions relating to political appointments, was about to intensify.

A few days later, in early February, claims of a falling-out between Carrie and Dominic Cummings reached the ears of some political reporters. Johnson was preparing to carry out his first Cabinet reshuffle since taking office the previous July. The reshaping of his administration had been nicknamed the St Valentine's Day Massacre by some newspapers because of the anticipated number of figures who might lose their jobs on 13 February, when the reshuffle was expected. Shortly beforehand, what were called 'Treasury sources' briefed newspapers including the *Daily Mail* that Carrie was backing ministers who believed Cummings's 'aggressive approach' towards ministers, officials and journalists was damaging Johnson. Cummings was believed to be behind a move to ban Lobby journalists from organisations he viewed as hostile to the government from attending a No. 10 briefing. He was also suspected of being instrumental in refusing to allow ministers to give interviews to the Radio 4 *Today* programme because of his belief that it was biased against the Conservatives. (Carrie is known to have favoured a softer approach to the media, which perhaps explains why Johnson had just written an article for *Grazia* magazine to mark the forthcoming International Women's Day.) The *Mail* reported:

> The rift has been fuelled by reports that Mr Cummings urged Mr Johnson to fire two ministers with close links to Miss Symonds: Chancellor Sajid Javid and Defence Secretary Ben Wallace. It is understood Mr Johnson has refused to sack Mr Javid in the reshuffle expected this week, but the fate of Mr Wallace is less clear.

There was more. The paper subsequently said that Cummings was also urging the dismissal of several special advisers and wanted Javid's own advisers to come under No. 10's authority.

Matters came to a head on the day of the reshuffle, 13 February. In fact, Ben Wallace stayed put as Defence Secretary, but Sajid Javid resigned from the government after refusing to bow to these third-party demands. He was replaced by Rishi Sunak. Having worked for Javid and known him well for several years, Carrie regretted his decision. Cummings appeared to have won the skirmish, but one source remembers clearly that at this point, Carrie seemed intent on fortifying her position. 'She was fixed on making a power grab,' says the source. 'And she wanted to get rid of Cummings and Cain.' What pleased her was that two of her former bosses had prospered. Zac Goldsmith, who had lost his seat in the Commons at the general election two months earlier and been given a peerage by Johnson, was allowed to continue in his job as an Environment and International Development Minister and given an expanded brief. John Whittingdale also returned to the government as a Culture Minister.

That weekend, Johnson and Carrie went to Chevening House in Kent to escape the rigours of London. They stayed there for the week of half-term because Chequers, the Prime Minister's official country retreat, was undergoing building work. Yet this decision ended up being frowned upon. On 15 February, Storm Dennis had caused serious flooding in parts of England and Wales. Unlike his predecessors, Johnson elected to stay put at Chevening instead of visiting those people whose properties and livelihoods had been affected in the most appalling ways. He was criticised for his lack of compassion. There was also surprise at his failure to attend five emergency Cobra meetings in London which were held in late January and early February to talk about the threat posed by Covid-19. There were doubtless many other calls on Johnson's time, but this was very high on the government's agenda. On other occasions, one source who has worked with Johnson was left wondering about the pressure on him: 'Time and again there are stories of Carrie demanding Boris's attention when he should have been doing other things. People would mumble under their breath, "Carrie wants him." Being Prime Minister is very demanding, but he was constantly being yanked out of meetings and so on because she wanted him.'

Yet there was another complication. Unwanted questions about who had paid for their Christmas holiday in the Caribbean were circulating. In keeping with regulations, Johnson had logged in the MPs' register of financial interests how much the holiday had cost – £15,000 – and named David Ross, the Carphone Warehouse co-founder and Tory donor, as having provided their accommodation. Yet Ross had subsequently told the *Daily Mail* that he had not paid for the holiday. Downing Street stuck to Johnson's line, meaning that to anybody but Ross, Johnson or Carrie, it appeared at the very least bizarre that he had denied being their patron when Johnson had claimed otherwise. This confusion eventually prompted an inquiry by the House of Commons Standards Committee, chaired by the Labour MP Chris Bryant. A second inquiry was conducted by the independent commissioner for standards, Kathryn Stone. Neither was resolved until July 2021, when it was established that Johnson had not stayed in Ross's villa, as originally thought, but had entered into an 'ad hoc arrangement' under which the Mustique Company, the island's management company, paid the owners of the villa in which Johnson and Carrie had stayed and Ross had subsequently reimbursed the company by lending them his villa. Johnson was cleared of wrongdoing but criticised for the haphazardness of his financial arrangements. In February 2020, however, the questions being put to Downing Street are said to have angered Carrie. 'Carrie would call the No. 10 press team and really lose her temper about the Mustique trip,' says a source. 'Some who worked there became very upset about the way they were spoken to. Tears were shed.' Johnson, too, was coming under greater pressure. He was even accused of being the 'part-time Prime Minister' because of his absences from Downing Street.

Scrutiny over the holiday coincided with the news on 18 February that Johnson and his estranged wife, Marina, had agreed to a divorce settlement relating to the division of money. This was reached at London's Central Family Court, where Judge Sarah Gibbons paved the way for Marina to apply for a decree absolute, meaning that the marriage would be ended legally. The details of the arrangement were not disclosed and neither Johnson nor Marina was in court. Documents show, however, that by this point several property transactions had taken place. In November 2019, the Johnsons' marital home in Islington had been sold for £3.35 million, an increase of £1.45 million on what they had paid for it fourteen years earlier. The next month, Carrie had sold her flat in Camberwell for £685,000 – just £10,000 more than she had paid for it the previous year. She is thought to have lost about £20,000 on the deal once stamp duty, legal fees and agents' fees are taken into account. Then, a few days before the court hearing permitting their divorce, Johnson and Marina unravelled their joint interest in their house in Thame. Land Registry records state that on 7 February 2020, Johnson bought it and an adjoining piece of land for £1.25 million. The property had two charges against it, from Barclays Bank and from Marina, suggesting that Johnson may have had to borrow from both the bank and Marina to complete the purchase.

Unsurprisingly, the divorce attracted press attention that Johnson and Carrie did not welcome. According to one source who worked in Downing Street at the time, Carrie had been 'lobbying pretty intensively' by this point to have her own special adviser. Johnson was told repeatedly by members of his team that such an appointment would be a bad idea as it risked becoming a distraction and would also go back on the pledge that had been made the previous July that Carrie would have no taxpayer-funded officials at her beck and call. They also wondered why she needed a personal adviser. One says: 'When Carrie's predecessor as prime ministerial consort, Philip May, had to do any media, which was rare, it was just handled by a No. 10 media spad. Carrie demanded her own PR.' Then, a compromise was reached. It was decided that Carrie could have her own adviser and their salary would be paid using Conservative Party funds. While it is unclear how Conservative Party members felt about their membership fees being used for this purpose, it did mean that a row over the use of public money was avoided. Sarah Vaughan-Brown, who had worked in senior positions at ITN and the Mirror Group, was considered the natural choice for this role, which came with a salary of about £100,000. The media was told that Miss Vaughan-Brown would assist Carrie in charitable work and on areas of special interest to her, including the environment, animal cruelty, combating violence against women and supporting the armed forces. As Miss Vaughan-Brown had recently set up her own firm, SVB Communications, some found it incongruous that the photograph of her accompanying the *Daily Telegraph*'s report of her elevation to Carrie's personal public relations adviser showed her a few days into her new job walking Carrie's dog, Dilyn, in St James's Park. Still, her expertise would be required within a couple of weeks.

On the morning of Saturday 29 February, a political row escalated in the full glare of public attention after the top civil servant at the Home Office, Sir Philip Rutnam, resigned and vowed to sue the government for constructive dismissal. In a statement which BBC news programmes broadcast that day, Rutnam claimed he had been the victim of 'a vicious and orchestrated briefing campaign' by allies of the Home Secretary, Priti Patel, whom he accused of failing to 'dissociate herself' from the attacks on him. This news did not reflect well on anybody. Within a few hours, Carrie and Boris had other, happier matters to share, though. That afternoon, Carrie posted a photograph on Instagram of Johnson kissing her on the cheek with a short statement revealing exciting news about their future together. 'I wouldn't normally post this kind of thing on here,' she wrote, 'but I wanted my friends to find out from me… Many of you already know but for my friends that still don't, we got engaged at the end of last year… and we've got a baby hatching early summer. Feel incredibly blessed.' Johnson would become the first Prime Minister to have got divorced and married in office since the Duke of Grafton in 1769.

The joy which emanated from Carrie was about to turn to thunder, however. On 11 March, *The Times* published a story on page 3, which is often home to humorous or colourful articles, under the headline 'Downing St dog to be reshuffled'. The report was accompanied by a large photograph taken a few months earlier of Carrie playing with Dilyn in the Downing Street garden. The paper claimed that Dilyn 'could be quietly rehomed before the couple have their first child in early summer'. It said that he had proved a 'sickly animal', with one source saying that Johnson and Carrie 'had already grown weary of the dog before they discovered that Ms Symonds was pregnant'. A particular bone of contention was the 'mess' that Dilyn had apparently created in their Downing Street flat. This source said: 'For a while there was dog shit everywhere in the flat.' Another source said that Dilyn was not the only mess-maker, with Johnson's own tidiness being questioned. The flat was described in the paper as being 'like a frat house' with 'clothes all over the place and takeaway cartons. The place was a mess.' It was also alleged that Carrie 'dislikes living in Downing Street and was the driving force behind the couple's decision to spend the recent half-term week at Chevening last month'. One source told the paper: '[Carrie] was fed up of being cooped up in a messy flat with the dog.' A Downing Street spokesperson denied that Dilyn was to be rehomed, but *The Times* published the information it had been given anyway. Little did they realise that this was the story which is said to have made Carrie angrier than any other. Early that morning, she took to Twitter to state: 'What a load of total crap! There has never been a happier, healthier and more loved dog than our Dilyn ... The people behind this story should be ashamed of themselves.' Seemingly, her own rebuttal was insufficient, however. She wanted to make this point even more emphatically.

Remarkably, it has been claimed that Carrie interrupted a high-level meeting in order to ask Johnson for his help in defending her corner. 'Carrie freaked,' says someone who worked in Downing Street at the time.

Boris was told he had to do something. It was funny because he had said openly to people previously that he hated Dilyn, but he was sent out to deal with this crisis. He was also furious. He told Lee Cain that a complaint would have to be made to the Independent Press Standards Organisation (IPSO). Cain told him this would be a mistake, but Johnson said: 'You don't understand. Carrie is really angry. And people love dogs. The public will turn against me if they think this is true.'

Cain is said to have told Johnson that on no account should IPSO become involved. Soon after dispensing this advice, though, Sarah Vaughan-Brown was asked to draft a letter to IPSO. Johnson and Cummings went through the proposed letter together when Johnson was suddenly struck by the reality of the situation. 'He put the letter down,' says an observer. 'He said: "We can't send this. It's ridiculous."' But having sided with his advisers, he then admitted in front of some of them: 'Carrie will go nuts. You don't understand what it's like upstairs.' Nobody wanted to become involved in his domestic affairs and the matter was left to lie.

The following year, in May 2021, Dominic Cummings gave evidence to a House of Commons select committee that was investigating the government's early response to Covid-19. His words then, delivered after the rush of events that took place, provide a further insight into this extraordinary row. In the days immediately before and after the story about Dilyn had appeared, countries around the world had begun instituting lockdowns. During his evidence session, Cummings said that 12 March, the day after the *Times* story appeared, was 'a completely surreal day'. He said that he sent a message to Johnson that morning warning him of 'big problems coming' because, in Cummings's opinion, the Cabinet Office was 'terrifyingly shit' and that between 100,000 and 500,000 people in Britain were going to die because of Covid. Cummings then told the select committee that all plans to deal with the growing threat presented by Covid were 'completely derailed' for two unconnected reasons. The first, he maintained, was that Donald Trump wanted the UK to 'join a bombing campaign in the Middle East'. The second was that Carrie was 'going completely crackers' over the story about Dilyn and 'demanding that the press office deal with that'. Cummings said:

> So, we had this completely insane situation in which part of the building was saying, 'Are we going to bomb Iraq?'; part of the building was arguing about whether we are going to do quarantine or not do quarantine; and the Prime Minister has his girlfriend going crackers about something completely trivial.

Despite the IPSO complaint never being sent, it does seem that Carrie managed to have the last word. In a show of strength which no doubt did something to pacify her, the article which had so offended her was removed from the *Times* website and has remained unavailable ever since. Few people of any standing could have insisted that one of Britain's bestselling and most influential newspapers bowed to their demands.

No doubt in need of a break after the saga of Dilyn, on 14 March Johnson hosted Carrie's baby shower at Chequers. About a dozen friends attended. Although Carrie had loved Chequers since first setting eyes on the place, Johnson is said to have always been slightly more circumspect about using it. This is because Prime Ministers have to pay out of their own pocket for any private entertaining that takes place there. Johnson was newly divorced; he had child maintenance to pay; and he was deprived of all sources of extra income from writing and speaking engagements. This meant he could rely on nothing more than occasional book royalties and his £160,000 prime ministerial salary. The timing of the baby shower was considered noteworthy by *Private Eye*. It pointed out that Johnson had given a press conference on Thursday 12 March in which he had said the growing crisis caused by Covid was now 'a global pandemic' and that 'many more families are going to lose loved ones before their time'. He stopped short of banning social gatherings at that time. Then, at another press conference on 16 March, two days after the baby shower, he said: 'Now is the time for everyone to stop non-essential contact with others and to stop all unnecessary travel.' Strikingly, he added that this was 'particularly important for people over seventy, for pregnant women and for those with some health conditions'.

By 22 March, Johnson and Carrie had relocated from Downing Street to Chequers. The next day, 23 March, Britain's first national lockdown began. Johnson continued to commute to Downing Street, though by 27 March he had tested positive for Covid and he isolated, alone, in the Downing Street flat. On 4 April, Carrie revealed on Twitter: 'I've spent the past week in bed with the main symptoms of Coronavirus. I haven't needed to be tested and, after seven days of rest, I feel stronger and I'm on the mend.' Within twenty-four hours, however, Johnson's condition had worsened and he was taken to St Thomas's Hospital in London. 'When Boris was ill, there was nobody in Downing Street to check he was OK,' says one long-term ally.

Carrie was elsewhere because she was pregnant. Boris was upstairs getting iller. It was only really [Conservative MP] Nadine Dorries who eventually said: 'Send for the chief medical officer, he is very ill.' That, for me, is the most extreme example of the absence of Marina. Nobody was there to look after him.

It must have been an agonising time for Carrie, of course. Johnson spent three nights in intensive care before returning to a hospital ward and at the time was considered lucky to have survived. He was released from hospital on 12 April and convalesced at Chequers for a short period before returning to Downing Street. Carrie took to Twitter to make her gratitude known. 'Thank you also to everyone who sent such kind messages of support,' she wrote.

Today I'm feeling incredibly lucky. There were times last week that were very dark indeed. My heart goes out to all those in similar situations, worried sick about their loved ones. I cannot thank our magnificent NHS enough. The staff at St Thomas' Hospital have been incredible. I will never, ever be able to repay you and I will never stop thanking you.

While Johnson recovered, he and Carrie were sustained by regular deliveries of food and wine from the organic farm shop Daylesford, owned by Lady Bamford, the wife of the Tory donor Lord Bamford. Indeed, they became regular customers there. It later transpired that they enjoyed £27,000 of food and drink, including takeaway meals, from this shop over the next twelve months.

Johnson was not the only key figure who was absent from Downing Street around this time. His chief adviser, Dominic Cummings, had left work on 27 March after his wife fell ill, subsequently left London with his family, and did not return until 13 April. He, too, suffered from Covid symptoms for much of this period. In the absence of Johnson and Cummings, it was left to the then Foreign Secretary, Dominic Raab, and the Downing Street communications chief, Lee Cain, to run the government machine. Carrie was shortly to have a baby, but one insider says they can recall learning that even then she tried to tell Johnson that Cain in particular was not doing a good job. 'There was a briefing operation going on against Lee. She told Boris he was doing badly, even though there was no evidence to support this idea. It was a way of undermining him.' On 29 April, politics was put aside by everybody when it was announced that Carrie had given birth to a baby boy. He was given the forenames Wilfred Lawrie Nicholas. Carrie took to Instagram to explain these choices. 'Wilfred after Boris' grandfather, Lawrie after my grandfather, Nicholas after Dr Nick Price and Dr Nick Hart – the two doctors that saved Boris' life last month,' she wrote. It was certainly a fitting tribute given her fiancé's health scare.

Over the next few months, the government-imposed restrictions on people's lives are said to have forced the Prime Minister into a more hands-on parenting role than he had perhaps expected to be in at the age of fifty-five. 'Boris had to change Wilfred's nappies,' reports one who knows him. 'I think Carrie expected him to share the domestic burden, even though he was the Prime Minister.' As it would turn out, she also wanted to share with Johnson some of the burdens of office.

CHAPTER 11

POWER STRUGGLE

As Boris Johnson regained his strength during the spring and early summer of 2020 following his brush with Covid-19, he was open to considering new ideas from his closest colleagues that might help to revitalise his government. It had been shaken by allegations that Dominic Cummings, his chief adviser, had breached rules implemented during lockdown by travelling 260 miles from London to County Durham. Cummings survived the controversy, but Johnson's decision to stand by him had used up vital political capital and, now barely a year into his tenure as premier, he needed to re-establish his authority. One proposal that was swiftly accepted as worthy of serious consideration sprang from the mind of Lee Cain, Johnson's communications chief, yet it was to lead to a serious row which ultimately had significant repercussions for Johnson's Downing Street operation. Carrie was at the centre of this battle.

Although Cain's own professional background is in newspapers, he had long felt that the existing model of presenting information to the media – holding twice-daily meetings behind closed doors with a civil servant taking questions from a group of accredited Lobby journalists – was steeped in the traditions of the twentieth century and geared specifically towards print reporters. Having seen how well the public had responded to the No. 10 press conferences that were held daily during the Covid-19 crisis, Cain discussed with Dominic Cummings the idea of hiring a spokesperson who would host regular White House-style press briefings instead. It was felt by them that these would bring Downing Street into the twenty-first century while opening up the Lobby system to a previously unknown level of transparency. Cain and Cummings are said to have been confident that they could sell this plan to Johnson. The only doubt in their minds was whether they should tell him. 'Lee and Dominic believed in this idea wholeheartedly,' says one who worked in Downing Street at the time. 'But they didn't know what they would do if Carrie found out about it. They were instinctively wary of her knowing about it too soon. They feared she might hijack the situation for her own ends.'

Cain and Cummings decided to risk it. They told Johnson in June 2020 and he liked the idea enough to encourage Cain to start drawing up plans. On 3 July, Johnson gave an interview to the radio station LBC in which he confirmed the initiative. It was subsequently explained that offices in 9 Downing Street, formerly used by the Chief Whip, would be refurbished and used for the briefings. A few weeks later, a job advertisement for this new post appeared on the Conservative Party's LinkedIn page, where it was described as a chance to 'communicate with the nation on behalf of the Prime Minister'. The chosen candidate would have to possess various attributes including 'excellent risk management and crisis communication skills'. They were told they would 'represent the government and the Prime Minister to an audience of millions on a daily basis, across the main broadcast channels and social media, and have the chance to influence and shape public opinion.' Some MPs were sceptical, regarding the scheme as too presidential for a parliamentary democracy, yet Cain pressed on. Careful thought was put into the enterprise. It was agreed with Johnson that short-listed candidates would face an interview and then hold a mock Lobby briefing in which civil servants would play the part of journalists. Finally, a focus group would give its opinion on which candidate had performed best. It was hoped that these tests would go a long way to guaranteeing that the best person would be chosen. The salary on offer was at least £100,000.

Despite the preparations, however, things went awry before the exercise was even fully underway. Allegra Stratton was a former political journalist who had worked for *The Guardian*, the BBC and ITV News before securing the job of communications chief to the Chancellor, Rishi Sunak, in April 2020. That Sunak was the best friend of her journalist husband, James Forsyth, had not been regarded as an obstacle to her moving into this important position, but she was said to be unhappy and isolated in the Treasury. One source remembers:

At the time, Allegra was working for Rishi Sunak. I don't know how much she liked it. When she heard about the new press spokesman job, she began paying visits to Carrie in the Downing Street flat. The next thing anyone knows, Carrie had begun telling Boris that Allegra should be his new press spokesman.

According to the source, Johnson asked Stratton to apply for the job formally and at a Chequers dinner attended by Sunak implied in front of his guests that she had got it, even though she had not yet been interviewed.

> Boris said something like: 'I hear you're going to be my new press spokesman.' Rishi Sunak was not at all happy. Allegra was basically offered the job without having to attend an interview and Lee told Boris this was a huge mistake. He kept telling Boris that the public had to genuinely like whoever his press spokesman was going to be, so it was important that the focus group had seen them.

A further complication was that other candidates had by this point applied for the job and been shortlisted. This source adds:

> Lee had to tell Boris that if he wanted to appoint Allegra, those other candidates' interviews would have to be cancelled out of courtesy. He was also reminded they had taken a risk in applying. Being seen as wanting to work for the Tories could be a very bad look for a broadcast journalist. Boris eventually agreed that every scheduled interview should go ahead and he said, 'Just make sure the best candidate gets the job.'

Yet it soon became clear that there was a sense of inevitability about the process.

Three candidates were shortlisted. The first was Ellie Price, a BBC political journalist. Angus Walker, a government special adviser formerly of ITV News, was also interviewed. And Allegra Stratton was the third candidate to make it through to the last stage. Although Stratton, like her competitors, had several years of experience as a broadcast journalist and had spent scores of hours delivering reports and taking part in discussions in front of live television cameras, her interview and mock press conference are said to have gone less well than those of her rivals. Indeed, one who was present when she was put through her paces says Stratton's overall performance was 'pretty poor'. By contrast, the same source says that Miss Price performed 'very well'. Walker was considered to have been 'reasonably good'. This account is backed up by a civil service document which was subsequently leaked. According to the document, the panel felt that Miss Price was 'calm, concise and authoritative where required – and that she showed the strongest appreciation of the opportunities and risks of [the] role and how it could be used to set the agenda'. The same document concluded that Stratton 'would need significant preparation and would therefore be a risky appointment'. It added: 'She took a firm and authoritative tone. At points this raised the temperature and made things more combative.' The source who was present says: 'Everyone said Ellie Price was the best person for the job. The focus group loved her. They felt she was trustworthy and they warmed to her. Nobody on the interview panel understood why Allegra had applied for the job because, despite being good on camera, she didn't seem very interested.'

Recorded clips of the journalists' performances are said to have been shown to Johnson along with the focus group's remarks. Despite Ellie Price being the clear favourite, however, he insisted that

Stratton should get the job. He was even heard to say when justifying his decision: 'When I said I wanted the best candidate for the job, I didn't mean I wanted the best candidate to actually get the job. I just meant Allegra had to get the job. Carrie will kill me if she doesn't get the job.' This account is supported by the aforementioned civil service document. At the time of Stratton's appointment in October 2020, Downing Street claimed there had been an open and competitive process. Yet the document confirms that the interview panel had recommended Price for the job.

After Stratton's appointment was announced, more difficulties arose. She allegedly asked for her own office in Downing Street, requested a higher salary so that her pay was in line with the £145,000 which Cummings, Cain and senior adviser Eddie Lister received, and insisted on the right to report directly to the Prime Minister. A source says:

> Lee Cain said no to all of her demands, so Allegra informed
> Carrie and then Boris rang Lee to question his decisions. Lee
> explained he felt Allegra's requests were unacceptable. Boris said
> he supported Lee and would tell Allegra she had to report to Lee.
> Allegra threatened to quit three times in one week and Lee told
> Boris he would find a way to make a bad situation work.

As had happened earlier that year when Carrie had asked for her own press adviser, a compromise was found. It was decided that Stratton's salary would be topped up using Conservative Party funds. Again, Conservative Party members were never consulted over this. Stratton is also said to have expressed her dismay at plans to bring Ellie Price in as her deputy. That idea was later dropped. In total, £2.6 million of public money was spent refurbishing 9 Downing Street to create a state-of-the-art press room, meaning that this very high-profile scheme attracted a lot of media attention. It is ironic to consider, therefore, that although Stratton held the position of Downing Street press spokesperson until April 2021, she did not give a single press briefing. The plan of having a press secretary was abandoned after Johnson went off it. 'Boris ditched the idea after civil servants told the No. 10 communications team that "people would die if Allegra was put on TV during a public health crisis",' says a source. 'Boris then listened to her contributions in meetings and quickly came to the same conclusions.' Stratton was later appointed a spokesperson for the 2021 United Nations Climate Change Conference, COP26, held that autumn in Glasgow. Nobody was under any illusion about the significance of her having been hired, however. Another of Carrie's demands had been met at the expense of one of Johnson's principal advisers.

Having helped to set up Stratton for the press secretary's job in mid-2020, there were other areas of special interest to Carrie at that time to which she is said to have drawn Johnson's attention with some success. One of these became public in early August 2020. It was reported that Johnson had shied away from enforcing a new government policy as a result of Carrie's intervention. Under Johnson's predecessor, Theresa May, measures had been put in place to make it easier for transgender people to change their birth certificates without a medical diagnosis. May had backed the idea that transgender people could self-identify as male or female and wanted to make it legally binding. Johnson's government had been preparing to overturn this move, but at the eleventh hour Johnson was said to have 'developed cold feet' after being 'influenced' by Carrie. An unnamed senior source told the *Mail on Sunday*: 'Many detect the hand of Carrie in this, but for whatever reason, Boris does not appear to have an appetite for this fight at the moment.' One well-placed source believes this report is credible. 'Carrie has quite a lot of gay friends, some of them work in government, and she has great sympathy for all issues relating to lesbian, gay and transgender people. She has certainly talked to Boris about this area of policy.' Indeed, two months later, at that year's Conservative Party conference, which was a virtual event because of the Covid-19 pandemic, Carrie was a judge of the LGBT+ Conservative group's lip sync competition. Johnson appeared with her briefly during the event, which was held on the Zoom videoconferencing system, prompting some to remark that he certainly appeared to have become more broad-minded since writing in a 1998 *Daily Telegraph* column of 'tank-topped bumboys'.

By this time, security concerns had been raised in Downing Street. One source says that suspicions developed that somebody other than the Prime Minister might have accessed classified documents which Johnson had to read and sign. The source says:

These documents would be left for Boris in red boxes. They would be taken up to the flat. Then something happened which led some people to think that somebody other than Boris might be reading them. These documents related – quite literally – to matters of life and death. They could not have been any more secret and were not meant to be seen by anybody else without full authorisation. A new system had to be thought up to get the documents to Boris without anybody else seeing them. Martin Reynolds, Johnson's principal private secretary, had to start taking them to Boris in person and then wait while he signed them.

None of this was made any easier by the fact that Johnson can display signs of paranoia himself. 'Boris trusts nobody,' says a source. 'And he can be overly suspicious himself.' This account is bolstered by a report in the *Sunday Times* that appeared in late January 2022. It stated that Dominic Cummings once went to the flat above 11 Downing Street and found 'highly classified "Strap" material, easily identifiable because it is printed on pink paper, lying around where it could be read by any visitor', while 'several of Carrie Johnson's friends had the access Pin code to the private flat above No 11 Downing Street so they could come and go at will'. Concerns about similar breaches at Chequers have also been raised, according to the *Sunday Times*.

Amid much advance publicity, Carrie, Johnson and Wilfred went for a week's holiday to Scotland in late August 2020. Regrettably, this 'staycation' trip was aborted after three days, supposedly for safety reasons, after a newspaper tracked them down to a remote north-west coast location overlooking the islands of Raasay, Rona and Skye. It did not help that a landowner called Kenny Cameron had also claimed publicly that Johnson, who had been given a tent by Carrie for his 56th birthday, had set up camp in his field without permission. Mr Cameron, a sheep farmer, told one newspaper:

Mr Johnson is meant to be leading the country and yet he is not setting a great example. Usually if people want to go inside a fenced area, they ask for permission first, but I was not asked at all. It is only polite to ask. He could have put up his tent in the garden of the cottage and there would have been no problem – but he didn't do that.

Soon after they returned to London, Johnson had some difficult decisions to face. By mid-September, he was told by government scientists that the Covid-19 virus was spreading again exponentially and there would shortly be an increased number of infections and hospital admissions. The summer lull in cases had come to an end. On 22 September, he announced that pubs would have to close at 10 p.m.; businesses that were not 'covid secure' would face five-figure fines or forcible closure; masks would have to be worn in more settings; and fines would be increased for those who did not comply. As part of the raft of new restrictions, office workers were also told to work from home. Having endured one national lockdown already, much of the British public felt miserable about the introduction of these curbs. Carrie, however, was not affected by the news in the most immediate sense. She was on holiday in Italy at the time with a group of friends and Wilfred. One photographer found her staying at the Grand Hotel Tremezzo near Lake Como, where rooms cost up to £600 a night. In the same week that Johnson told the nation of the limitations under which they would have to live, Carrie and her friends were seen enjoying a late-night supper. Among the group was Aline Nassif. Miss Nassif's presence puzzled some who know her. Although she and Carrie had both worked as special advisers to John Whittingdale until 2016, Miss Nassif had made no secret of the fact that they had fallen out. 'I know that Aline was very upset by Carrie,' says one source who knows them. 'It's very difficult to understand the dynamic of their friendship but I have seen Aline in tears because of Carrie, so I have never understood why she went on that trip.'

Another who was present on the holiday was Nimco Ali. A couple of weeks later, it was revealed that she had secured a new job advising the Home Office on tackling violence against women and girls. This government role, for which she was being paid £350 a day for about two days' work a month, attracted comment because it had not been advertised but was instead a direct appointment. Furthermore, the job appeared not to have existed prior to Miss Ali taking it on. A Home Office spokesperson later insisted to journalists that hiring an individual directly was 'appropriate for short-term advisory roles, for example to lead a government review or to champion a specific subject area'. The spokesperson added: 'As this is a direct appointment, the role was not advertised and was not offered to anyone other than Miss Ali.' How Miss Ali came to be appointed to a job which was never advertised has never been completely clear. One source says that by this point, serious discussions had also taken place as to whether Miss Ali could join the House of Lords. These came to nothing.

What most people were unaware of at the time that Miss Ali joined the Home Office was that a couple of weeks earlier – and just a few days before she went on holiday with Carrie – she had accepted an invitation from Carrie to be Wilfred's godmother. Wilfred was baptised amid great secrecy by Fr Daniel Humphreys in the Henry VII Lady Chapel at Westminster Cathedral. Some found it unusual that Miss Ali, a Muslim, had taken on this role in Wilfred's life, yet the Catholic Church only insists that one godparent is a baptised Catholic. (Carrie and Johnson are both baptised Catholics, although as a schoolboy Johnson was confirmed into the Church of England.) Incidentally, another of Wilfred's godparents is believed to be Alex Wickham, now the editor of the political newsletter Politico London Playbook, a daily bulletin about British politics that is considered by some Lobby journalists to be at least as important as the BBC Radio 4 *Today* programme. It is not known whether Miss Ali or Wickham have ever declared to their respective employers their link to the Prime Minister.

Nimco Ali was not the only person known to Carrie whose professional progress featured in the press in the autumn of 2020. So, too, did that of Richard Holden. Yet in his case, it would perhaps be more accurate to say that it was his *lack* of professional progress that became a talking point. As described in Chapter 6, in the spring of 2018 Carrie had given evidence against Holden at Southwark Crown Court after he was accused of sexually assaulting a Tory aide. He was found not guilty of the allegation and allowed to leave court without a stain on his character. By late 2020, Holden had been elected as a Tory MP and in November word went round Westminster that Mark Spencer, the Tory Chief Whip, had recommended that he should join the government as a parliamentary private secretary to a Cabinet minister, the first rung on the ministerial ladder. Shortly afterwards, however, the *Daily Mail* reported that Holden's promotion had been blocked by Johnson because he feared that Carrie 'would disapprove'. It was further claimed that

Holden, who had worked successfully on Johnson's 2019 leadership campaign, had already been barred by Johnson from joining the No. 10 press team the previous year for the same reason. Despite being popular and well-regarded, Holden has remained on the back benches ever since.

Around the same time, there were separate claims in the *Daily Mail* about one of Carrie's closest friends, Ross Kempsell. As outlined in Chapter 7, Kempsell had been invited to play tennis with Johnson since the summer of 2018. The *Mail* believed he was to be given a senior job in Conservative Party headquarters, supposedly on a salary of about £90,000. Though it was denied at the time, this story turned out to be accurate. Kempsell had alternated between journalism and politics for several years. In July 2019, he left TalkRadio to become a policy adviser to Johnson in the 10 Downing Street Policy Unit. A year later, he left Downing Street and went to work as a reporter on the newly launched station Times Radio. By early 2021 – as the *Mail* had predicted – he had been installed as the Conservative Party director of research. Iain Carter, who had done the job until then and whom, as described in Chapter 6, Carrie is said to have disliked, left. These various manoeuvres allowed an unhealthy view to form in the minds of some Westminster figures that appointments were being made in an unconventional way.

Throughout this period, Johnson, of course, was having to juggle the considerable problems of running the country when every element of life was under strain in a way that had been unknown in Britain since the Second World War – and all in the same year that he had endured an expensive divorce, had a near-death experience and become a father again aged fifty-five. Yet he still found time for public appearances which the couple considered to be important. The following week, for example, he and Carrie made a joint televised address to mark the *Daily Mirror* Pride of Britain awards. They praised the medical professionals who had done so much for them during 2020 and nominated nurses Jenny McGee and Luis Pitarma for an award after they cared for Johnson at St Thomas' Hospital. They also nominated the maternity team which had delivered Wilfred. In the message, Carrie said:

> You continue to provide care for all of us in the very toughest of times and it's because of you that not only is Boris still here, but that we are proud parents to our sweet baby boy. As a family we have so much to be thankful to the NHS for and we will never stop being grateful.

Johnson added: 'Exactly right. So I want to pay thanks to the utterly brilliant team at St Thomas' Hospital who saved my life.'

By the time of this television address, the atmosphere inside No. 10 was close to boiling point. Dominic Cummings had already told Johnson in the summer of 2020 that he intended to leave his job on 18 December. In the event, he walked out of Downing Street as Johnson's chief adviser for the last time five weeks earlier than that, on Friday 13 November, after relations between them broke down. Cummings has always said there were several reasons for his departure, one of which was Carrie. He felt that she had been plotting the removal of his allies and so he quit. He elaborated on this in a BBC interview broadcast in July 2021 in which he said: 'I thought that his girlfriend was interfering with appointments. She wanted to have people fired and she wanted to have people promoted in ways that I thought were unethical and unprofessional. And that also led to a big argument between [me and Johnson].' When asked what his evidence for this claim was, he cited the series of events which led to Allegra Stratton being named as Johnson's press secretary in October 2020 as an obvious example.

He went on:

Carrie's view was and is: 'The Prime Minister doesn't have a plan and he doesn't know how Whitehall works. Someone is going to set a lot of the agenda. It can either be the civil service, or it can be Dominic and the Vote Leave team, or it can be me.' In 2019, her view was: 'Better that it's Dominic and the Vote Leave team than the civil service, because that's the route to winning and staying in No. 10'. As soon as the [2019] election was won, her view was: 'Why should it be Dominic and the Vote Leave team? Why shouldn't it be me that's pulling the strings?'

He added:

In fact, literally immediately after the [2019] election it was already clear that this was a problem. Before even mid-January [2020] we were having meetings in No. 10 saying, 'It's clear that Carrie wants rid of all of us.' At that point we were already saying that by the summer either we'll all have gone from here or we'll be in the process of trying to get rid of [Johnson] and get someone else in as Prime Minister ... The situation we found ourselves in is that within days the Prime Minister's girlfriend is trying to get rid of us and appoint complete clowns to certain key jobs. So do you just go, 'OK that's fine' or do you say, 'That's a disaster, we should try and avoid that happening'?

Lee Cain, who is widely regarded as having been more loyal to Johnson than any of his other advisers, left Downing Street on the same day as Cummings. Cain's departure came as more of a surprise. For one thing, Johnson had offered him the job of chief of staff after Cummings had told him that he was going to leave. This plan had the support of many influential people in Downing Street, not least Johnson's long-term adviser Eddie Lister and Simon Case, the Cabinet Secretary. At Johnson's request, Cain went to Chequers one Wednesday evening to see him to discuss this promotion. He had with him a four-page document which he had written setting out the various reforms that he – as chief of staff – believed would have to be made in order for Johnson's government to prosper. His ideas included appointing a new Chief Whip, reforming Conservative Party headquarters, and the total overhaul of Downing Street's political operation. It came as a surprise to Cain to discover that Carrie was also at Chequers and decided to sit in on his meeting with Johnson. Yet she, in turn, seemed unaware that Johnson had asked Cain to succeed Cummings. It was only when Cain mentioned it that she realised what was going on. After Cain had presented his ideas, Johnson courted him for the next two weeks. Ultimately, Cain asked for forty-eight hours to think about the offer.

During this 48-hour thinking period, on 10 November 2020, *The Times* contacted Downing Street asking if it was true that Cain was about to be promoted. Johnson is said to have reacted angrily and demanded to know who had leaked the story. Downing Street sources have always insisted that it was not Cain. 'It was not in Lee's interests to leak news of his potential promotion,' says one. 'He was still pondering whether to accept the job. So why would he leak it? He could have just accepted the job and asked the press office to put out an official statement. The leak was clearly designed to damage him.' On 11 November, the story appeared on the front page of *The Times* under the headline: 'Boris Johnson to give Vote Leave ally Lee Cain key No 10 role in shake-up'. At 8.02 a.m. that day, the Politico London Playbook, edited by Carrie's friend Alex Wickham, posted an 800-word bulletin about Cain's mooted new job. In it, Wickham wrote: 'Playbook can reveal there are serious doubts as to whether the move will happen. One senior government special adviser insisted that "no decision has been taken," that the PM has not even begun the interview process for the job, and that they do not believe Cain will get it.' It went on: 'Playbook received WhatsApp messages from no fewer than nine serving special advisers last night, asking if it was true and expressing their bewilderment.' There were further insights, including that Cain's promotion would lead to resignations, each of which appeared to scotch the idea that Cain would get the promotion. It appeared to be a subtle but significant strike against Cain. That it was written by one of Carrie's closest friends who is also, to boot, the godfather of Johnson's youngest son did not escape some people's attention.

When Cain read the article, he walked into Johnson's office and shouted at him in front of shocked colleagues. 'I'm ashamed of you!' he yelled. 'I'm disgusted in you.' He then slammed the door.

Johnson, who is known to dislike confrontation, panicked. Later that day, he reinforced his offer. But Cain told him that he could not accept it, explaining that he did not trust Carrie. To this, Johnson is said to have replied: 'Fuck Carrie!' He begged Cain to stay. Their conversation was interrupted when Johnson was told that the Queen, with whom he spoke weekly by telephone, was on the line. Cain left the room. When he returned half an hour later, Johnson had his head in his hands. He said: 'Are you briefing against Carrie?' Former colleagues recall Cain telling them that it was then he realised that nothing would ever change, he could not continue working for Johnson, and he must resign. Having done so, he recommended that he should be replaced by James Slack, which he eventually was.

On Cain's final day at Downing Street, he and Johnson chatted warmly and posed for a photograph together. Cain made it clear to him that there were no hard feelings on his part. As he packed some belongings into a cardboard box, he heard music by ABBA booming from the flat upstairs. Carrie was apparently hosting what was later described as a 'victory party', despite the fact that the country was in lockdown at this point. This alleged event would later be brought to the attention of the Metropolitan Police. Anonymous press briefings followed in the days afterwards in which Cummings and Cain were portrayed as having an 'abrupt' management style which was not popular with some Downing Street staff. *The Times* acknowledged that although their departure appeared to have been agreed with Johnson, some believed the two men had 'emerged as the losers in an extraordinary power struggle with Carrie' and that their leaving 'represents a victory for Ms Symonds and Allegra

Stratton'. On 14 November, the paper even published a leading article on the matter. '[Carrie] has found herself at the centre of the soap-operatic political storm engulfing Downing Street,' it stated.

> She appears to have played an instrumental role in demanding the immediate departure from No 10 of Dominic Cummings, Mr Johnson's chief adviser, yesterday. His exit became inevitable after she had vetoed the appointment of Lee Cain, head of communications and a long-time acolyte of Mr Cummings, as chief of staff to the prime minister. Ms Symonds is alleged to have plotted the Vote Leave pair's downfall in the flat above No 11 with Allegra Stratton, the prime minister's new spokeswoman, who will host a daily televised press conference.

It concluded:

> As long as Ms Symonds is in Downing Street, she will have Mr Johnson's ear. The departure of Messrs Cain and Cummings offers what has so far been a chaotic premiership the chance to reset and impose order. But whoever replaces them would be wise not to make an enemy of Ms Symonds.

One person who had a bird's eye view of the twists and turns that took place within Downing Street throughout 2020 believes that this assessment is fair. 'At the point that Dom and Lee were thinking of leaving, Boris found himself standing at a crossroads,' this person says.

He had two choices. He could have persuaded them to stay to carry on the job they'd started together, or he could go Carrie's way, which Dom and Lee and others felt was the easy way. Boris chose the easy way. Their departure marks the moment when he lost control of everything. Many feel it was a mistake.

On 19 December 2020, Johnson was accused of 'cancelling Christmas' after he implemented new lockdown measures affecting one third of England's population. Under these laws, people in the south-east and east of England, together with the population of London, were not able to mix with other households at all during the festive period. These measures were initially put in place for two weeks. Many people probably assumed that Johnson and Carrie would, like most families who lived together, therefore be spending Christmas alone, with their eight-month-old son Wilfred. They were wrong. In October 2021, there was widespread surprise when it came to light via an article in *Harper's* magazine that Nimco Ali had also been with them in Downing Street over Christmas. A No. 10 spokesperson's justification for this was that Miss Ali was part of Carrie and Johnson's so-called 'childcare bubble', a little-known loophole which allowed people from different households to mix on Christmas Day 'but only if reasonably necessary for the purposes of childcare and where there are no reasonable alternatives'. At the same time as Miss Ali completed the couple's 'childcare bubble', some found it odder still that Carrie's mother, Josephine, who lives alone in East Sheen, just a few miles from Downing Street, seemingly spent that Christmas – her grandson's first – without her only daughter. When it first became known publicly that Miss Ali had been in Downing Street during the Christmas of 2020, she stated on Twitter that she had received 'two days of racist and disgusting tweets' after it was wrongly alleged that she had breached lockdown rules when she had not. As it turned out, Miss Ali's presence in Downing Street would not represent the only gathering to be held there during the Covid crisis that prompted comment later on.

CHAPTER 12

BUYER'S REMORSE?

The early part of 2021 brought with it new opportunities for Carrie. In late January, it was announced that she had been hired to work as the head of communications at the Aspinall Foundation, which breeds endangered animals such as rhinos and cheetahs in captivity in Britain before releasing them into their natural habitat. As described in Chapters 7 and 8, Carrie had links to this charity and its chief, Damian Aspinall, stretching back to at least the autumn of 2018 and had encouraged Johnson's interest in its work as well. In early 2019, she and Johnson went together to one of its sites in Kent and he subsequently wrote about it in glowing terms in the *Daily Telegraph*. On the face of it, this job appeared to be perfect for her, combining her love for animals with her skills as a publicist. It was even reported that she would be able to carry out her duties from Downing Street while her mother, Josephine, helped to look after Wilfred, who was by then nine months old.

Shortly after this announcement, however, it came to light that questions about the financial arrangements of the Aspinall Foundation were being asked at an official level which might have troubled any other incoming communications director. Since December 2019, the Charity Commission, the independent regulator of the charity sector, had been investigating concerns about its management of conflicts of interest plus what has been described as 'a related-party transaction'. By March 2021, these concerns had been elevated to becoming the basis of a statutory inquiry examining the administration, governance and management of the charity by its six trustees. There was a particular focus on its financial structure, including questions about why Damian Aspinall was living in a Grade II-listed thirty-room Palladian mansion on one of its sites in Kent but paying only £2,500 a month for the privilege.

Thanks partly to the charity now employing the Prime Minister's girlfriend, there was further press scrutiny. The foundation's six trustees were soon identified. Damian Aspinall is the chairman of the board. His daughter, Tansy, is another trustee. The third is Ben Goldsmith. As explained in Chapter 7, he had introduced Carrie to some of his contacts at Bloomberg Philanthropies, leading ultimately to her working for the campaigning organisation Oceana in 2018. Ben Goldsmith's half-brother, Robin Birley, is the fourth Aspinall Foundation trustee. In 2019, he donated generously to Boris Johnson's Tory leadership campaign and is also the owner of one of Carrie's favourite haunts, the Mayfair private members' club 5 Hertford Street. The fifth trustee is a financier called Maarten Petermann. Charles Filmer, a wealth manager and contact of Carrie's close friend, Zac Goldsmith, is the sixth. Zac Goldsmith was himself a trustee of the Aspinall Foundation until the summer of 2019.

The Charity Commission's inquiry, which was still active at

the time of this book going to press, was also set up to consider whether the Aspinall Foundation's trustees have complied with and fulfilled their duties and responsibilities under charity law. Such an investigation is not embarked on lightly. While there is no suggestion that Carrie is a subject of this investigation, it is undoubtedly the case that since early 2021 the Aspinall Foundation has had to devote a portion of time to accounting for itself – sometimes publicly – rather than promoting its work with animals. Despite this, Carrie has stuck by the charity while also remaining an adviser to her previous employer, Oceana. Bearing in mind that her connection to the Goldsmith family certainly did no harm to her chances of securing the job at the Aspinall Foundation, which was not advertised, her loyalty to the Goldsmiths may go some way to explaining her decision to remain employed there.

In early 2021, some commentators developed other theories about why Carrie had re-entered the world of paid employment at all. Indeed, the notion that it was in fact *necessary* for her to earn a salary because of Johnson's alleged cash-flow problems became a popular one. Then, by coincidence, just as the Charity Commission's interest in the Aspinall Foundation was deepening, Simon Walters of the *Daily Mail* revealed extraordinary details of another story involving another charitable exercise. This time, though, Carrie was at the centre of it. The newspaper's investigation concerned the hugely expensive remodelling of the Downing Street flat where Johnson and Carrie lived – a refurbishment programme that Carrie had overseen. This sparked a controversy that lasted for months. It is only now that there have been two official inquiries into what has become known as 'Wallpapergate' – one by the Electoral Commission and the other by Johnson's own standards adviser, Lord Geidt – that the facts of the story are clearer.

Like Tony Blair, David Cameron and Theresa May before him, when Johnson became Prime Minister in July 2019, he opted to live in the larger premises above 11 Downing Street rather than the smaller flat above No. 10. Although it is known as the 'No. 11 flat', it occupies three storeys and is, in effect, the equivalent of a house minus the ground floor. Successive occupants since 1997 have chosen to decorate it according to their own taste and have had access to an agreed amount of taxpayers' money to do so. For several years that figure has been set at £30,000. Should a Prime Minister wish to spend more than that sum, they must pay the difference, as David Cameron did when he funded part of a makeover that took place after he entered Downing Street in 2010.

In March 2021, the *Mail* claimed that Johnson was secretly trying to set up a charity to help pay for the redecorating programme that Carrie had embarked upon shortly after moving into Downing Street in July 2019. Johnson believed this enterprise had spiralled 'totally out of control', in the words of one source. The newspaper disclosed that the designs of an environmentally conscious interior decorator called Lulu Lytle and her company, Soane Britain, had inspired the project, including 'gold wall coverings' costing £840 a roll. The *Mail* stated that Johnson had asked a Conservative Party donor, Lord Brownlow of Shurlock Row, to run the charity. Officially, it would raise funds to preserve for the nation several areas of 10 and 11 Downing Street, including the state rooms. Yet some sources had revealed to the *Mail* that they believed the proposed charity's true use would be to take over the funding of the works that Carrie had recently overseen, thereby easing Johnson's financial burden.

After the *Mail*'s largely accurate report was published, the Conservative Party contacted the Electoral Commission seeking advice on an 'urgent query relating to donations'. This led to the commission's investigation. Its subsequent report, published in December 2021, revealed that between June 2020 and February 2021, at least £112,549.12 was paid to Lulu Lytle in relation to the redecoration of the No. 11 flat, including the purchase of furniture. Lord Brownlow funded all of this expenditure. But whereas just over half of this sum was paid to Miss Lytle by Lord Brownlow directly, £52,801.72 of it came via a more complicated route which, it transpired, breached the Political Parties, Elections and Referendums Act 2000. There is no suggestion that Lord Brownlow realised this when he made the donations. Rather, he relied on Downing Street's advice.

The Electoral Commission discovered that in May 2020, Lord Brownlow was asked to set up a trust for the purpose of the refurbishment (in fact, the trust was never established). Two months later, the Cabinet Office paid £52,801.72 for work that had been done on the flat by that time. This money was then reimbursed by the Conservative Party. In October 2020, Brownlow in turn reimbursed the Conservative Party the same amount – £52,801.72 – effectively cancelling the debt. He made a party donation of £15,000 at the same time. Legally, the total that Brownlow therefore paid to the Conservative Party on that occasion – £67,801.72 – should have been logged as one political donation. Yet the £52,801.72 of Brownlow's payment which covered the cost of the Downing Street refurbishment was not reported as a donation to the Electoral

Commission. This resulted in the Conservative Party being fined £17,800 by the Electoral Commission. The Labour Party, together with other opponents of Johnson, interpreted this as an example of his having a very distant relationship with telling the truth.

Nobody involved emerged well from this wrangle. Ultimately, Johnson was forced to do what he had sought to avoid all along and pay the £112,549.12 which the works cost. Having dragged on for months, the affair had also been politically damaging to him. Moreover, the Conservative Party suffered by association, appearing to have allowed itself to become involved in a scheme which did not pass what is colloquially known as 'the sniff test'. And another casualty was Lord Geidt, Johnson's standards adviser. He had published a report in May 2021 that concluded Johnson had not broken the ministerial code over the funding of the renovations. Yet when, in January 2022, WhatsApp messages sent from Johnson's mobile phone to Lord Brownlow were published as a result of the Electoral Commission inquiry, even more questions were raised about whether Johnson had told the full truth about the affair. Lord Geidt wrote to Johnson, expressing his dismay. Johnson was then forced to offer a 'humble and sincere apology' for not having given Lord Geidt these WhatsApp messages at the time of his inquiry. He blamed the lapse on security issues which had forced him to change the phone from which the messages were sent.

Apart from the WhatsApp messages casting doubt on Johnson's initial account of the episode, they had the further effect of raising questions about where Johnson's priorities lay. The first WhatsApp message was sent at lunchtime on Sunday 29 November 2020 from

Johnson's phone to Lord Brownlow. It read: 'Hi David, I am afraid parts of our flat are still a bit of a tip and am keen to allow Lulu Lytle to get on with it. Can I possibly ask her to get in touch with you for approvals? Many thanks and all best, Boris.' It is worth emphasising that Sunday 29 November was a politically challenging day for Johnson, making it all the more remarkable that he had time to concern himself with Lulu Lytle's redecoration of his flat. Records show that on the same day he also wrote a letter – his second of that weekend – to backbench MPs who were close to rebelling over plans to introduce new Covid restrictions. When all of this came to light, some people quite naturally wondered why the Prime Minister was pestering a businessman for money when he might have been expected to be fully focused on these more important matters.

Indeed, it is worth saying that Johnson is not known for his interest in interior design. If anything, it seems he would be more likely to share the view of an earlier Downing Street resident, Norma Major. In *The Goldfish Bowl*, the book by Cherie Blair and Cate Haste about prime ministerial spouses, Mrs Major revealed that when she and John Major moved there in 1990, she waited until 1993 to update the accommodation – even after a terrorist attack made it distinctly unhospitable. 'We lived with the holes in the ceilings and the torn curtains – the result of the IRA mortar attack in 1991 – for eighteen months,' she recalled. 'You obviously wouldn't walk in and expect to change it just because it wasn't to your taste,' she went on, 'but it ought to at least be a suitable residence for the Prime Minister.'

There is no question that the cost of the works on the flat came to preoccupy Johnson. One Downing Street source says they can remember him holding meetings about the upgrade during 2020 when his staff expected him to be tackling Britain's myriad problems. 'I couldn't believe that while the country was crippled by the Covid crisis, Boris was spending his time on this stuff,' says the source. 'Some people just walked out of these meetings because this really had nothing to do with government business. I was incensed, frankly.' It seems relevant to point out, however, that his interest was primarily focused on the cost of the works rather than the works themselves. For the allegedly hard-up Johnson, who was emerging from an expensive divorce while starting a new family and deprived of any income beyond his £160,000 prime ministerial salary, the issue of who would pay for the upgrade seemingly became all-consuming. Carrie's thoughts on the matter have never been aired publicly.

Following the departure in late 2020 of Dominic Cummings and Lee Cain, as discussed in Chapter 11, attention in the spring of 2021 turned to the atmosphere in the 'new' No. 10 and Carrie's apparent grip on the operation. Having helped to force Cummings and Cain out, her influence was felt by many to have grown. The introduction of a Covid vaccine and the unveiling of a 'road map' for ending the lockdown pointed to the smooth running of the government machine, and the Conservatives had a sustained poll lead over Labour at the time. Yet behind the scenes, Westminster watchers believed there were tensions. In late February 2021, more questions about Carrie's control were asked after a civil servant named Oliver Lewis resigned as the head of No. 10's Union unit, a job in which he was responsible for trying to prevent Scottish independence. Lewis, who had been head of research at the Vote Leave campaign under Dominic Cummings, had been in post for just two weeks. His surprise exit was explained by his friends as the result of his feeling his position had become untenable. There were suggestions, notably repeated in *The Times*, that Carrie had accused him of briefing against Michael Gove, then the Cabinet Office Minister.

At about the same time, Carrie was the subject of a profile in the magazine *Tatler*. Appearing on the front cover under the headline 'Carrie's Coup: inside the world of the most powerful woman in Britain', the piece mentioned that Eddie Lister, one of Johnson's closest political allies who had left Downing Street in January 2021, had been 'alienated' by the 'power broker' Carrie. This piece soon became infamous for its reference to a 'visitor' to Downing Street talking about the 'John Lewis furniture nightmare' that Carrie and Johnson are said to have inherited from his predecessor, Theresa May. There is no record of Carrie ever saying these words herself, yet she was soon dubbed 'Carrie Antoinette' on social media platforms for her perceived snobbery. The vitriol became too much for her. Before long, she turned to her former boss John Whittingdale for help. 'One of the stories which she did get really upset about was when she was alleged to have made some disparaging remark about John Lewis,' Whittingdale says.

> She was very upset because it was completely untrue and she loves John Lewis. I can remember being asked if I could get a message to Sharon White, who was running John Lewis, because Carrie wanted to say it's so untrue. She does take stories about

her personally. She finds it quite difficult. I did get the message to Sharon White. I knew her because she'd run Ofcom [when I was Culture Secretary].

Soon after, the *Daily Mail* alleged that Carrie had apparently damaged the careers of two leading civil servants. One of them, Antonia Romeo, was said to have been a strong contender to become the first female Cabinet Secretary until Carrie supposedly launched into an angry tirade and made personal insults about her. Johnson subsequently appointed Simon Case as his new Cabinet Secretary, despite a common perception that Case was a less experienced candidate than Romeo. The newspaper also said that Carrie had targeted Helen MacNamara, a former property and ethics chief at the Cabinet Office, after she had refused to authorise expenses for refurbishing the Downing Street flat. The *Mail* suggested that Carrie had tried to persuade Johnson to remove Miss MacNamara. Even if this is true, however, it is a fact that Miss MacNamara chose to leave her job in order to take a senior post with the Premier League.

At the same time as these reports surfaced, some of Carrie's closest friends were settling into their new jobs as top aides to Johnson. All are seen as modernisers, some of whom learned their trade working as special advisers to government ministers. One was Henry Newman, who was once described by Carrie as one of her 'favourite people'. He became a senior adviser to Johnson, having previously worked for Michael Gove at the Ministry of Justice. Another was Simone Finn, a former girlfriend of Michael Gove. She was recruited as Johnson's deputy chief of staff, Dan Rosenfield having become chief of staff in January 2021. Finn was better known by some in Westminster as the host of Carrie's 30th birthday party in March 2018. Their appointments meant that there were five so-called 'Goveites' in key jobs in No. 10, the others being special advisers Henry Cook and Meg Powell-Chandler and political secretary Declan Lyons, who is engaged to Carrie's close friend Sophia True. All three are roughly the same age as Carrie, and Cook and Powell-Chandler are longstanding friends of hers. Newman, Cook and Powell-Chandler are even said to be referred to by Johnson as his 'three musketeers'. One source says:

> Boris suddenly found himself surrounded by Carrie's friends. It's a funny situation because he now hangs around with a much younger gang as a result. Someone who had dinner at No. 10 told me Carrie was with her young friends and Boris came and said hello to everyone and Carrie wanted someone to take a photograph of her and Boris together. It was all quite 'performative'. That's the word that was used.

Some of these appointments and departures even led the long-established Conservative think-tank the Bow Group to call for an independent investigation into Carrie's 'powers over government'. In late February 2021, the group's chairman, Ben Harris-Quinney, said:

> She currently holds no official role in the Conservative Party or the government, yet consistent reports in the press suggest that Ms Symonds is taking a central role in running the country, without any authority or accountability to do so. She has not

been elected, she has not been appointed, she holds no legal or constitutional powers to make decisions relating to who should hold government posts, to be party to privileged information, or to set the policy direction of the country. It is therefore urgent that a review and inquiry takes place to determine what Ms Symonds' role in the governing of the United Kingdom is, and has been to date.

Some of Carrie's closest friends leapt to her defence. The Conservative MP Tracey Crouch told *The Times* she disliked the way Carrie had been portrayed as a Lady Macbeth figure. 'I think it's a bit sexist,' said Crouch. 'I also think it's really rude to Boris.' She suggested that Britain should explore creating a formal role for Prime Ministers' partners. 'I think it's really interesting whether or not we think of setting up something similar to the first lady in the States,' she said. Another Conservative MP, Laura Trott, told the BBC that any briefings against Carrie were 'distasteful'. She said: 'I used to work with Carrie, she's an incredibly talented and able person and I think there should be some consideration given about whether some of these things would be said about a man.'

One person who saw things differently was Dan Hodges, a columnist on the *Mail on Sunday*. In April 2021, he wrote a withering article headlined 'Britain Votes for Prime Ministers – not their partners. Boris needs to get unelected, unaccountable Carrie to back off'. In it, he stated that 'it's an open secret within Westminster how Ms Symonds's influence extends over government'. He continued:

Ministers attempt to appease her and her whims, because they know it's the only way to keep their careers on track. Journalists appease her for fear of being ostracised by the No 10 communications team she helped build. Or because they benefit personally from her briefings. Or because they fear the cabal of sycophants she surrounds herself with will turn on them, and issue one of their ritualistic denunciations of 'sexism'. But worst of all is the way the Prime Minister of the United Kingdom continues to appease her.

Hodges added that tolerance of her operating without any accountability was 'a national scandal'. He wrote:

> Team Carrie needs to disband. The 'friends' need to go. The unofficial press operation needs to go. The lobbying on policy, appointments and strategy needs to stop. And the next roll of wallpaper needs to be paid for out of her own pocket, not from some Tory fat cat. Because if these things don't happen, then it won't be Ms Symonds who ultimately pays the price. The nation will.

To this, Carrie's friend, Zac Goldsmith, was quick to respond in her favour. 'This really is classic Dan Hodges/Mail,' Goldsmith wrote on Twitter on the day of the article's publication. 'Completely fabricate a bunch of stories about someone, and then use those fabrications to pour hate and bile on them. And dunk the whole thing in 1950s sexism.' Yet one source who knows Johnson well and who has encountered Carrie on many occasions observes a pattern which backs up what Hodges had to say. Indeed, they say the irony is that Goldsmith's own counterattack surely fits the narrative that Hodges was pushing. This source says:

> Anyone who falls foul of Carrie is immediately accused in the media either of having briefed against her or of being a misogynist. It's always the same. The fact is, she has achieved power through patronage. The only way she was ever going to get into Downing Street was as the plus-one.

Carrie's former boss John Whittingdale disagrees. The influence Carrie is claimed to have is inaccurate, he says.

> She wasn't involved in the [September 2021] reshuffle and to some extent it was because they were so concerned it would be branded the Carrie reshuffle. The fact I lost my job is surely proof of that. Henry Newman and Simone Finn are close to her, yes. I'm sure Boris and Carrie discuss things in a way that previous spouses would not because they were much less political. Samantha Cameron had little interest in politics. Philip May didn't have a great knowledge of politics. This is the first time the PM's wife has themself been a committed political activist and had knowledge and experience of working in politics, so of course it's going to be talked about. But she's very good. She advised me for fifteen months, so I know she's good.

He adds:

She gets a tough time. It upsets her and I feel sorry for her. It's a pretty lonely existence. I think they've struggled. She doesn't see as much of Boris as she'd like because he's trying to run the country. She's also had to put up with vicious press campaigning against her, some of which has been ridiculous and has upset her. She saw what happened to me, but that's not the same as when you experience it yourself.

While Westminster watchers reflected on Carrie's apparent political influence during the spring of 2021, she was busy organising a top-secret event that must have seemed to her to be infinitely more important and which had nothing to do with politics whatsoever: her wedding. The fact that Carrie and Johnson had married only became known publicly when the press was told about the ceremony hours after it had taken place at Westminster Cathedral on Saturday 29 May. Although Johnson had been divorced twice, Carrie was able to become the third Mrs Boris Johnson in this august setting because the Roman Catholic Church allows divorcees to remarry if their previous marriages did not take place in a Roman Catholic church. The ceremony was officiated by Fr Daniel Humphreys, who had baptised their son, Wilfred, the previous year. Two of Carrie's friends, Janna Lawrence and Cat Humphrey, acted as witnesses. Johnson became the first Prime Minister to marry in office since Lord Liverpool married Mary Chester in 1822.

Only thirty guests were invited, the maximum number of attendees allowed under Covid restrictions in England at the time. Six weeks later, these restrictions were eased. In view of tensions about the relationship in Johnson's own family, some have said privately that they believe his getting married while these rules remained in place worked to Johnson's advantage, as a large-scale and very public wedding which some of his closest relations might not have attended could have proved embarrassing for him. Some of his siblings, including Rachel, are thought to have been at the ceremony, along with his father, Stanley, and his half-sister, Julia. Yet his four children by Marina are not thought to have attended the event. Images were released to the media after a reception had taken place in the garden at Downing Street. One photograph showed Carrie wearing a white lace gown and a garland of white flowers in her hair with Johnson by her side. In another, she was barefoot, and bunting and hay bales were visible in the background.

Somebody briefed a selection of newspapers a few days later that, in a show of thrift, Carrie had rented the wedding dress she wore for a mere £45. Her asceticism attracted much media comment, yet even the couple's wedding reception did not escape the scrutiny of some journalists who had grown increasingly suspicious of Johnson and his reluctance to spend his own money. The day after it took place, the *Daily Mail* website noted that a marquee had already been installed in the No. 10 garden for 'charity events' up to two weeks before the marriage. It was claimed that the marquee had been used in the days running up to the wedding 'for official functions', prompting questions as to whether Johnson and his guests had also used it and, if so, whether he had contributed to its cost. Downing Street refused to comment.

The newly married couple did not go on a honeymoon. Instead, they were soon due in Carbis Bay in Cornwall for the G7 summit, which Johnson was hosting and which was held between 11 and 13 June. For Carrie, this marked a significant moment. For the first time in two years, she was a prime ministerial spouse rather than simply a girlfriend. The only other major summit that had been held since Johnson had become Prime Minister in July 2019 took place in Biarritz in August 2019. Carrie did not attend it, citing work commitments. On home turf, however, she was expected to play the role of hostess, leading a 'spousal programme' alongside the main G7 conference. On 10 June, she and Jill Biden, then aged seventy, had tea together while Johnson and President Joe Biden held talks ahead of the summit. Later, the two political wives were pictured on a beach with Wilfred while Johnson and Biden spoke to journalists. Carrie took to Instagram to inform her thousands of followers of the day's events. 'Wonderful to spend some time this afternoon with First Lady Dr Jill Biden at Carbis Bay,' she wrote. 'We even dipped our toes into the water. Beautiful but freezing!' Meanwhile President Biden caused some amusement by explaining to a group of reporters: 'I told the Prime Minister we have something in common. We both married way above our station.' Johnson responded: 'I'm not going to dissent from that one. I'm not going to disagree with the President there or indeed on anything else...' Johnson later appeared to underline his commitment to feminist causes by telling the group of world leaders in his opening speech that, post-Covid, 'we will build back better, greener, fairer and in a more gender-neutral and perhaps a more feminine way'. Few understood what this would mean in practice.

The following month, Carrie revealed that she was pregnant again, choosing this moment to disclose some other sad personal news. 'Hoping for our rainbow baby this Christmas,' she wrote on Instagram.

> At the beginning of the year, I had a miscarriage which left me heartbroken. I feel incredibly blessed to be pregnant again but I've also felt like a bag of nerves. Fertility issues can be really hard for many people, particularly when on platforms like Instagram it can look like everything is only ever going well. I found it a real comfort to hear from people who had also experienced loss so I hope that in some very small way sharing this might help others too.

Many women's groups appreciated her openness and honesty, and she was praised for using her position to discuss this most delicate matter.

In late August, however, Carrie found herself embroiled in further controversy, this time in an international context, as American and NATO forces withdrew from Afghanistan. Among the thousands of Afghans fleeing the war-torn country were the staff of an animal sanctuary called Nowzad which had been founded in 2007 by a former British soldier. It cared for animals affected by the war. After Kabul fell on 15 August 2021, Western forces had to help thousands of Afghans who had cooperated with them during the war get out of the country or face likely death at the hands of the Taliban.

Nowzad's staff decided that they, their families and as many animals as possible should leave at the same time. A Nowzad representative asked the British government for help, but the Defence Secretary, Ben Wallace, made it clear in television interviews that he was not prepared to 'prioritise pets over people'. Nowzad soon secured private funds to charter a plane and, with ninety-four cats and sixty-eight dogs, its staff made for Kabul Airport only to be told they could not board due to a last-minute change in visa requirements. The next day, 28 August, Nowzad's boss, who is British, returned to the airport with the animals alone. This time, he was able to board a 230-seat plane, though he was the only passenger; he says he offered seats for other evacuees and that the animals travelled in the hold. His staff crossed the border to Pakistan the following month and later made it to Britain. A major publicity campaign was established during this period which kept the media spotlight fixed firmly on Nowzad, ensuring the issue became something of a cause célèbre. During this period, Ben Wallace complained to MPs that the issue had diverted resources on the ground away from saving people more in need of rescue.

In December 2021, this evacuation of Kabul returned to the news pages after a junior Foreign Office official, Raphael Marshall, published a dossier he had submitted to the Foreign Affairs Committee of the House of Commons in which, among other extraordinary revelations, he claimed that the decision to let Nowzad's animals leave Afghanistan potentially put British troops' lives at risk and prevented Afghan translators from fleeing – claims Nowzad disputed in their evidence. He also said he believed Nowzad's staff would have faced no danger from the Taliban if they had remained in the country. In light of this, Johnson was asked again about the episode. He denied having anything to do with Nowzad's exit from Afghanistan. It soon transpired, however, that his parliamentary private secretary, Trudy Harrison, the MP for Copeland, had offered to assist with Nowzad's evacuation.

In a letter dated 25 August 2021, Harrison said she had received confirmation from the Foreign Office, Home Office and Ministry of Defence that Nowzad's animals would be allowed to travel to the airport to leave on a charter flight. She said the Defence Secretary, Ben Wallace, had made it clear that all sixty-nine members of Nowzad's staff and their family members would also be able to board an RAF flight. Downing Street insisted that Harrison had acted in her capacity as a constituency MP, rather than as Johnson's parliamentary private secretary, but since nobody who worked for Nowzad at that time was a constituent of Harrison's, it was certainly considered unusual that she had written this letter. And Dominic Dyer, who, as mentioned in Chapter 9, is a friend of Carrie's, later told the BBC that he had lobbied Johnson and Carrie. 'I forced the Prime Minister's arm, I think all of us behind this campaign did,' he said, adding: 'I have no doubt Carrie Johnson gave him a hard time.' In a separate interview with LBC radio, Dyer also said: 'Obviously I knew Carrie Johnson, I made clear my concerns to her, no doubt she spoke to [the Prime Minister].' Asked whether he had gone directly to Mrs Johnson, Dyer said: 'Yes, yes. Carrie Johnson took the message forward, not just through me but through the Conservative Animal Welfare Foundation.'

Whatever the degree of input Carrie had in persuading the British state to ease the passage of Nowzad's staff and the animals from Afghanistan, she chose to involve herself in yet another controversial matter at the Conservative Party's annual conference held in Manchester in early October 2021. It was revealed to the media in advance of the conference that Carrie would be making a speech at a drinks reception held in partnership with the LGBT charity

Stonewall. At the time, Stonewall had come in for significant criticism from a variety of high-profile gay people including one of its
founders, Matthew Parris, over its stance on transgender people.
Parris accused Stonewall of becoming 'tangled up in the trans issue'
and 'cornered into an extremist stance' which ultimately raised questions about freedom of speech. Stonewall's chief executive, Nancy
Kelley, had also sparked criticism after likening 'gender critical' beliefs – the belief that a person's biological sex cannot be changed – to
antisemitism. A number of organisations, including Ofcom and the
Equality and Human Rights Commission, had withdrawn from an
employers' programme run by Stonewall because of its 'hardline'
position on transgender rights. Under the Diversity Champions
programme, members pay Stonewall to examine the way their organisations operate, looking at policies such as who can use their
lavatories and the use of personal pronouns in the workplace.

In her speech, which was watched by Johnson and his sister,
Rachel, Carrie insisted that Johnson is 'completely committed' to
LGBT rights. 'There are still those who tell me that being LGBT+
and a Tory is somehow incompatible,' she said. 'Well, looking
around me tonight, we can see that is blatantly untrue.' She added:
'The idea that your sexual orientation or gender identity should
determine your politics is now as illogical as saying your height or
your hair colour should.' She pointed to her husband's support of
same-sex marriage and his vote to repeal Section 28 almost twenty
years earlier and said that he had appointed a 'special envoy' on
LGBT+ rights, adding: 'I want you all to know that we now have
a Prime Minister who is completely committed to accepting those
gains and extending them further.'

Many felt that Carrie had entered into territory that was perhaps unwise for the wife of a Prime Minister, yet few spoke out openly. The following month, however, Nikki da Costa, who had stood down as Johnson's director of legislative affairs in August 2021, told *The Times* that she believed some of Johnson's closest advisers were allowing the government's policy on trans rights to be dictated by Stonewall. Miss da Costa also claimed that he was being presented with 'skewed' advice by a powerful lobby in No. 10 that was undermining women's rights. She alleged this included deciding what Johnson saw in his red boxes and refusing to arrange meetings with people who would present opposing views. 'There is no other organisation – no business, or charity, no matter how big – that can pick up the phone to a special adviser sitting outside Boris Johnson's office and get that person to speak directly to the Prime Minister,' she told the paper. 'But that is the kind of access that Stonewall has. I've never seen that in any other circumstances in Downing Street.' Miss da Costa did not name individuals, but *The Times* stated that Johnson's senior adviser, the previously mentioned Henry Newman, had 'supported the role of Stonewall's diversity training programme in government'. Miss da Costa also said: 'The PM is not receiving the range of opinions on the debate around gender identity that he should. It is a result of a very small group of advisers being able to control what goes in the Prime Minister's box and the advice he sees.' In view of Carrie's speech at the recent party conference, some cited da Costa's account as another example of Carrie helping to facilitate policy decisions which were at odds with what many in the Conservative Party believe. One source says: 'There has been a lot of anger within the Tory Party, especially among women, on this issue particularly. That Carrie has involved herself in it has never been helpful.' It should be said that in February 2022, just hours after excerpts of this book appeared in a serialisation in the *Mail on Sunday*, it was announced by Downing Street that Henry Newman would be leaving his job there and going to work for Michael Gove.

The following month, it was Johnson's turn to irritate some in his party. Having hosted the COP26 climate change summit in Glasgow, at which he warned of the dangers facing the planet and instructed attendees to stop 'quilting the earth in an invisible and suffocating blanket of CO2', he boarded a chartered private plane and flew back to London. His reason for wanting to return to the capital so quickly was that he had been invited to a gathering of former *Daily Telegraph* leader writers at the Garrick Club. This was a gift to his opponents, who immediately labelled him an arch-hypocrite for not practising what he preached.

Worse was to follow for Johnson, however. He was one of thirty-two guests at the Garrick Club dinner, some of whom had worked on the newspaper as far back as the 1970s. Notably, Carrie's father, Matthew Symonds, who, as mentioned in Chapter 1, was a *Telegraph* leader writer in the 1980s, was not invited. Two weeks after the event, on 17 November, a pro-EU weekly publication called the *New European* published a story suggesting that one of Johnson's fellow guests had relayed to it a comment Johnson had made that night which is said to have upset Carrie enormously. The newspaper's report stated:

The New European has been told that the Prime Minister was asked how family life with his new wife and mother to his child Carrie Symonds was going. His reported answer, that he was experiencing 'buyer's remorse' over the union, astonished some of those present ... While many found the Prime Minister's remark amusing, others were uncomfortable and astonished he should be so indiscreet in such broad company. One dinner guest told *The New European*: 'Clearly he just assumed he was amongst friends, but it was a remarkable thing to say and there were a number of raised eyebrows around the table.'

At 10.30 on the night that the *New European*'s story surfaced, a Downing Street press officer, believed to be the director of communications, Jack Doyle, rang its editor in chief, Matt Kelly. He told Kelly the story was untrue, defamatory and that Johnson would be taking legal action against the newspaper. Astonishingly, Kelly was not the only person to receive this message. Late that night, Doyle also contacted Nick Moar, a nineteen-year-old digital media specialist who set up a news aggregation service called Politics For All when he was seventeen. Politics For All took the top lines from the news articles of various websites and posted them across social media, pointing readers to the original publication. Having clocked up about 500,000 Twitter followers, including many MPs, it was considered a clever idea and a great success. Moar had seen the *New European*'s story when it broke and tweeted: 'BREAKING: Boris Johnson has reportedly stated he is experiencing "buyer's remorse" over marrying Carrie Johnson.' He was at a nightclub when Doyle rang him and told him to delete the tweet or face legal action. Moar later recounted that he knew Carrie paid attention to Politics For All's Twitter page because she had once 'liked' one of its posts and then immediately 'unliked' it. He did not delete the offending tweet; nor did he – or the *New European* – ever face legal action. Oddly, however, Moar's Twitter account was abruptly suspended in January 2022, prompting him to take legal advice over how it could be reinstated.

What is clear is that on the night the *New European*'s story was published, the press operation within No. 10 swung into action in a way that it very rarely does, barring a major crisis. One source says that as well as Doyle contacting Matt Kelly and Nick Moar, somebody else from Downing Street contacted and cross-examined at least one person who attended the Garrick Club. This source says:

> Boris made the buyer's remorse comment, almost certainly as a joke, to a couple of people who were sitting close to him at the Garrick. It seems the *New European* reported it rather more seriously than was merited. But the point is that Carrie can be very sensitive when it comes to what's written about her. A hunt ensued to find out whether Boris had really said this and then to find out the identity of the *New European*'s source.

Another source says: 'The full weight of the Prime Minister's press office is and always has been put into protecting Carrie. I know that to be true.'

What several sources also insist is true is that Carrie has what has been described as a group of 'favoured journalists' through whom she communicates – and, on occasion, via whom she admonishes anybody who is thought to have slighted her. One source with close knowledge of this aspect of her character says:

Several people who have written profiles of her have been rung up out of the blue by Carrie's friends and offered 'help'. This is not normal. Her network in the media includes a small group of journalists who are her acolytes. They claim she's not interested in politics. I don't believe it. She's very political. She thinks she shouldn't be written about, but she is powerful. She's clever. If you're writing about her, she doesn't contact you directly. Instead, one of her acolytes will say something to you at a party or something like that. One of her best weapons is her ability to cut people out of things, particularly anything to do with the Lobby. The way she operates is that if you're on side, she's fun. If you're not, it can be vicious. Her great power is that she has these men around her who she can control.

During the research for this book, two well-established national newspaper journalists revealed that, having written about Carrie in factual but unflattering terms, they bizarrely received expletive-ridden and highly intimidating messages which were sent from the mobile phone of one of these journalists. To prove this, some of these messages were read out. They were, indeed, what might euphemistically be called 'direct'. To say any more than that would identify those on the receiving end of the messages, but these two journalists – who do not know each other – have no reason to lie. Other contributors have told stories about two very well-known public figures who have been reduced to tears after Carrie remonstrated with them for having said or done something which upset her. And in the latest edition of Tom Bower's biography of Boris

Johnson, *The Gambler*, it was reported that Carrie's temper has had devastating consequences for at least one person she believed had behaved inappropriately. 'Carrie had run-ins with female civil servants in particular,' Bower wrote. 'One at Chequers had caused her special anger after Dilyn, [the Johnsons'] terrier, had also created a problem. The housekeeper complained that Dilyn was chewing furniture and had damaged a valuable book. After heated discussions between Boris and Carrie, the housekeeper was fired the following morning and the dog survived.' Bower received no complaint over this version of events when his book was published, but when I approached Downing Street for comment as this book was going to press, a spokesperson for Mrs Johnson said: 'This is absolutely not the case and I can only presume someone is briefing against the dog again.'

One person who knows Boris Johnson very well, both politically and personally, has given much thought to the development of his character over the past four or five years. This person is in no doubt about what has happened. 'Boris changed after he met Carrie,' they say.

He always was a bit of a lonely figure because he has few friends, but now it's worse than ever. He's fallen out with his children, he's lost Marina, and since he became Prime Minister so many of the problems he's had to deal with have been because of Carrie. Deep down, I think he knows this. I've seen him make excuses before to avoid going upstairs to his flat in Downing Street because he doesn't want to be with her. The whole thing is like a Greek tragedy. He wanted power, he got power, but it came at a price. He could've been a great Prime Minister, but his lack of discipline, which led him to get involved with Carrie, has cost him. His potential to transform the country has been squandered and, as far as I'm concerned, it's because of her. Whereas before he had some people he trusted working with him, now he's surrounded by Carrie's cohort and a few civil servants. It's like a toxic relationship. He's isolated. It's very sad. Politically, there is no agenda; he's just drifting. One of the key things for me is that his family call him 'Al', because his real name is Alexander, but Carrie calls him 'Boris', which is what he's known as publicly. Few people see 'Al', but everyone sees 'Boris'. I wonder whether Carrie calls him 'Boris' because 'Al' hasn't let her in yet, meaning she doesn't know him as well as you might expect.

Another person who knows Johnson and Carrie well, having worked with both of them during his own lengthy political career, says that the reality of their marriage may be more difficult than some people realise. 'I don't think Carrie has many friends,' says this person. 'Nor does Boris. He has fewer, in some ways. She's had a lot to put up with. I don't think Boris is close to his family at the moment, so they both have few really close, loyal, personal friends. Maybe that was something they found in common.'

If it is true that their relationship can be described as a meeting of two people who may be more emotionally vulnerable than the majority of the British electorate appreciates, only the hardest of hearts would fail to recognise the sadness of this fact. We can hope that they find sufficient stability to ensure that the lives of their children, Wilfred and Romy, who was born in December 2021, are happy and straightforward. Yet the troubling question that, perhaps, too few people in Westminster and in Fleet Street have dared to ask publicly is what effect their perceived weaknesses have had on the way Britain has been governed since 2019. One of Johnson's closest allies in the Cabinet has said privately to sources quoted in this book that they believe Carrie is 'the number one problem' in Johnson's administration. Given that Carrie is unelected and unaccountable, many voters will wonder whether it would be better for the country if the Cabinet minister in question had the courage to tell the Prime Minister this to his face.

AFTERWORD

When I embarked on this project in the summer of 2021, I could have had no idea that just a matter of months later Carrie Johnson would find herself accused by an increasing number of people of being involved in a series of scandals which threaten to derail her husband's premiership. At the time of going to press, the Metropolitan Police are investigating a string of parties which were allegedly held on Downing Street premises during the Covid-19 lockdowns of 2020 and 2021. They include one gathering which supposedly took place in November 2020 in the Downing Street flat where she and Boris Johnson live. If this allegation is proven, it would constitute a breach of the very rules Johnson himself implemented and could result in a penalty fine. I find this state of affairs somewhat staggering, but, then again, much of what I have learned about Carrie Johnson has surprised me.

Her move aged twenty-two from the world of public relations to politics was certainly not anticipated given that she had shown little interest in the workings of Westminster up until then. Still, her rise from Conservative Party press officer to ministerial special adviser and then to Tory communications chief aged twenty-nine certainly suggested a hunger to succeed as a vital cog in the party machine. And yet it now seems clear that her heart wasn't really in it. Within months of taking up that latter post in 2017, she tried unsuccessfully to get a new job advising the Foreign Secretary – one Boris Johnson. Their relationship began soon after. Then she lost her job at Conservative Party headquarters after being accused of fiddling her expenses and taking too much holiday.

As of early February 2022, the police are looking into what has been dubbed Partygate, in which she may have been a significant player. This comes after Wallpapergate, in which she was instrumental. It also follows the outrage expressed over Nowzad's animals being rescued from Afghanistan at a time when many felt that all efforts should have been focused on rescuing the Afghans most at risk. Some who lobbied for the evacuation of these animals have spoken openly of her close interest in that particular matter. Collectively, these matters point to a deeper problem from which Carrie cannot escape scrutiny.

It is important to emphasise that Carrie's courage and determination have, in the past, been in evidence. Nobody can doubt her commitment to causes close to her heart, such as animal welfare – an interest which I share. Her campaign against the release from prison of the serial sex criminal John Worboys, who drugged her in the back of his taxi when she was nineteen, was admirable. In taking such a strong stance, she was effectively working against the decision of a Conservative government while employed by the party. Her decision to waive her anonymity as a victim and talk about her experience at the hands of Worboys was similarly brave.

And her openness and honesty in being willing to discuss a miscarriage in 2021 is also rightly praised.

Yet complaints against her exist because of her apparent desire to exercise power and patronage without accountability. Her friends have often dismissed criticism of Carrie as simply sexist, but this won't do. For one thing, to scrutinise Carrie's actions in Downing Street is not to excuse Johnson himself from taking ultimate responsibility for how power is exercised. But scrutiny of people in positions of power is not a zero-sum game. There is surely space in the public debate for the investigation of both. For another thing, her actions have adversely affected people's careers, not least those of other women. And, most importantly, the questions at stake are too important to be brushed aside. Many of the sources who contributed to this book have kept their stories about Carrie private until now. Some even said they were motivated to talk because they concluded that it was in the public interest to do so. All believed that it was better that the facts as they know them were set out openly.

My intention in publishing this book is not to destabilise Boris Johnson in his capacity as Prime Minister. I want him to govern to the best of his abilities. Yet while I know that the buck stops with him, the evidence I have gathered suggests his wife's behaviour is preventing him from leading Britain as effectively as the voters deserve. This should matter to everybody.

INDEX